Here is a rich and varie 
ordinary, bizarre and e
in the pages of *The T*
years. Stephen Winkw
funnier sequel to the
Times.

In this new volume you
tax on bachelors, the cal ... ince of Lincoln, the hundred-year-old tin of roast veal, the invention of the first crash proof aeroplane, the death of Rin-Tin-Tin, and Paxton's 11-mile glass building; you will also discover how bank notes were forged in prison, why Russians do not shave, how J. B. Priestley's views on white and brown eggs created an international furore, how the oldest man in the world took up flying lessons and, at last, how that famous headline 'Small earthquake in Chile – not many dead' first originated.

This is compulsory reading for all serious students of ephemera. It is rich in human interest, full of fascinating, amazing, entertaining and startling information – but above all, this is *The Times*, so it is true!

Also published by Unwin Paperbacks

THE FIRST CUCKOO
Letters to *The Times* 1900–1980
chosen and introduced by
Kenneth Gregory

THE SECOND CUCKOO
A new selection of letters
to *The Times*
chosen and introduced by
Kenneth Gregory

AMAZING TIMES
The most amusing and amazing
articles from *The Times*
chosen by Stephen Winkworth

ACCIDENTAL TIMES
Bizarre stories from *The Times*
of the Victorian era
chosen by Jane Lambert

MORE AMAZING TIMES!

a second selection of the most amusing and amazing articles from

Chosen by
STEPHEN WINKWORTH
illustrated by **ffolkes**

London
UNWIN PAPERBACKS
Boston Sydney

First published in Great Britain by George Allen & Unwin 1985
First published by Unwin Paperbacks 1986

UNWIN ® PAPERBACKS
40 Museum Street, London WC1A 1LU, UK

Unwin Paperbacks
Park Lane, Hemel Hempstead, Herts HP2 4TE, UK

Allen & Unwin Australia Pty Ltd.,
8 Napier Street, North Sydney, NSW 2060, Australia

Unwin Paperbacks with the Port Nicholson Press
PO Box 11–838 Wellington, New Zealand

British Library Cataloguing in Publication Data

More amazing times : a selection of
extraordinary, bizarre and funny articles
from The Times 1918–1983.
1. Anthologies
I. Winkworth, Stephen II. The Times
082 PN6014
ISBN 0–04–827153–5

Printed and bound in Great Britain
by Cox and Wyman, Reading

INTRODUCTION

One generally comes across old newspapers in attics, cellars and woodsheds, in among the kindling and the spiders. In common with wine and firewood, they improve with age. Their contents mature, and as the living sap of news dries out they become a better read. Not infrequently the destinies of all three are linked, for reading scraps of old newspapers before consigning them to the flames is one of the joys of lighting a wood fire, and the joy is all the greater if a glass of wine goes with it.

Reading yesterday's news is a pleasure that can easily assume the proportions of an addiction. As Robert Louis Stevenson wrote of Joseph Finsbury:* 'A taste for general information, not promptly checked, had soon begun to sap his manhood. There is no passion more debilitating to the mind.' Where better to indulge such a passion than in the archives of that most amazing newspaper, *The Times*?

The following selection was made at the debilitating expense of actually reading, or browsing, through sixty-five years of *The Times*. For safety reasons, this was not done before an open fire; however, since this quantity of newsprint contains something over two and a half billion words, or the equivalent of forty thousand average length novels, considerable fortitude was required. Wine – in what exact quantities it is now unnecessary to recall – undoubtedly helped in the process of compilation, and may be thought by come to add to the enjoyment of perusal, for these articles are all ephemera. There is scarcely anything about Politics, World Events, or the Tide of History. Entertainment – preferably amazing – laced with the occasional laugh and the very occasional shudder: that is what *More Amazing Times* is all about.

* In *The Wrong Box*.

Although great pains were taken to avoid raising historical dust, let alone adding to it, unfortunately it must now be admitted that all this research has unearthed, or rather shaken loose, one awkward fact. A persistent story about *The Times* concerns a headline which is said to have been composed by Claud Cockburn – SMALL EARTHQUAKE IN CHILE: NOT MANY DEAD. He claims to have won a prize for it, as the dullest of the day. On the occasion of the most recent earthquake in England (19 July 1984) Calman's front-page cartoon compressed it to SMALL QUAKE: FEW DEAD. Its fame has died hard. The original of such a renowned item of trivia seemed worth tracking down for this collection; nor would it appear at first sight a very difficult task. Earthquakes, like executions, hoaxes and monkeys, have their own separate entries in *The Times Index*, and are further subdivided by region.

Cockburn's headline will be found on page 68. Alas, it is a fake. The two-line story is genuine, but appeared as an untitled paragraph in a column headed TELEGRAMS IN BRIEF. The famous headline is altogether absent from the archives of *The Times*.

It is true that there are a great many reports of earth tremors in Chile during the twenties and thirties. Most are indeed very boring and have suitably boring headings. Possibly editorial opinion was more seismologically inclined in those days. Certainly in retrospect Chile appears to have been a troublingly unstable place in which to live. But none of the headlines on the subject quite fits. Take, for example, plain EARTHQUAKE IN CHILE. Uncommon, but not rare, as a collector would say. One such story ends with the words 'no persons were injured', but SMALL is lacking, and in no case is there a subheading. In place of SMALL we find ANOTHER, MORE, SLIGHT – but never in a Chilean context. In the only South American example of such wording, the belittling, hand-in-front-of-the-mouth impact of ANOTHER – in this case, ANOTHER EARTHQUAKE IN PANAMA – is quite spoiled by the somewhat alarming subheading ISLAND REPORTED MISSING. A notable occurrence of SLIGHT was the SLIGHT EARTHQUAKE AT MANCHESTER (May 1931), which had an interesting and helpful side-effect for a golfer, whose ball, trembling on the very edge of its hole, was just shaken in to win the match. But Manchester is not Chile.

The only remaining repository of earthquake news is the column of brief news flashes on the Imperial and Foreign News page, headed TELEGRAMS IN BRIEF. A number of these appear to fulfil the necessary requirements of fact, location and date. A little detective work soon eliminated all but one, and this does stand out as a quite superbly uninteresting piece of news. It mentions two unheard-of places in one short sentence, pedantically insists that one of these unheard-of places is to the north, and the other to the south, and ends by saying that nothing of any importance happened – 'no damage was done'.

Is it not reasonable to suppose that the competition was actually for the most boring Foreign Telegram? Great intellectual effort was devoted to the things; in fact, Cockburn tells of one subeditor who took a two-line Reuter's telegram off to the Athenaeum and worked on it until ten in the evening before handing it in. Besides, there are conflicting reports of what went on in Room 2 at Printing House Square in those days. Graham Greene was working there as subeditor at about the same time as Cockburn, and remembers a competition to spot unintentional *double entendres*, won by the headline BLOCKING IN HYDE PARK – though to a modern ear this might have done for either prize. As for the exact wording, it must be remembered that Cockburn was the supreme myth-maker of the thirties, and his memory has always been famous not so much for photographic accuracy as for vividness. Those fine, throwaway words 'Not Many Dead' are missing, but they have always been suspect – would Chief Subeditor Anderson, under Geoffrey Dawson, have tolerated anything so flip and callous? 'No damage was done' says it all, and more boringly.

One of the least earth-shaking headlines ever printed in

The Times appeared in 1970 – EIFFEL TOWER STANDING UP WELL. But there are other boring headlines the reader may wish to ponder before falling asleep. Quite a frequent one in the thirties and forties was THE OLDEST CLERGYMAN. The porridge on many a rectory sideboard must have chilled to a lump while the household digested that piece of gerontological gossip. Almost as thrilling was COMPOSITION OF POTATOES – AN INCONCLUSIVE INQUIRY (April 1919), compared with which FALL OF A BRANCH IN ROTTEN ROW (May 1928) sounds positively eventful. On a more exotic note there is MARKET GARDENERS OF BULGARIA – A MIGRATORY CALLING, while for pure euphony SUPPOSED GASSING OF HIPPOPOTAMUSES wins the Savannah Palm. The headline FOG appeared at least twice between the wars, but it was not *The Times* which committed the absurd solecism FOG IN CHANNEL – CONTINENT ISOLATED. It is alleged to have been the *News Chronicle*, but once again the searchlight of scholarship may evaporate this myth.

As for TELEGRAMS IN BRIEF, they too were capable of considerable stylistic variation, achieving at times a most untelegrammatic lushness:

> Monsignor Kyrillos III Basileion, Archbishop of Cyprus, is sending a petition, signed by His Beatitude in the vermilion ink which he is privileged to use in virtue of a rescript issued by the Emperor Zeno, to both Houses of the Imperial Parliament, asking that Cyprus be united to Greece. – February 1929.

A name such as Kyrillos III Basileion would appeal to the Firbank in any reporter; nor would such tendencies have met with much opposition from an editorial staff which, in a leader a few years earlier, had referred to a goat as a 'horned quadruped of the genus Capra'. But this was a prime period for names, and particularly for long and impressive ones. Owners of the more resounding species of double-barrelled name have nowadays a regrettable habit of discreetly dropping the part before the hyphen. It is, of course, bad taste to joke about people's surnames, but the editor feels that his own has been taken in vain often enough to allow him a certain licence. Appellations such as 'Old Greshamian, Sir Weldon Dalrymple Champney' must have been something of a burden to carry through life, and 'A. fforde-Tipping' must have had one or two jokes made at his expense, as must the coroner, Mr Bentley Purchase. Another coroner still remembered among his profession is Dr Ingleby Oddie – a name many a detective writer of the thirties must have wished they had invented. Mr Gentle-Cackett will, I hope, forgive a gentle cackle or two as the price of his appearance in a newspaper of record. Did that famous army vet, Sir Francis Duck, ever meet General Sir Bindon Blood (who should clearly have refused promotion above Brigadier), and if so, would not the meeting have made an admirable subject for the brush of the painter Frank Spenlove Spenlove? It is by no means impossible that big-game hunter Marcuswell Maxwell was entertained during his travels by Sir Gordon Guggisberg, Governor of Guiana, and perhaps other guests at the dinner table included Osmonde Grattan Esmonde, or that pioneer aviator Sir Bartram ('Bartie') Rumble.

All these people did something with their lives to earn the attention of readers of *The Times*, as indeed did another learned man with a splendid name – Dr Farquhar Buzzard, physician to George V, expert on 'the art of thinking', and Freudian scholar. What would Dr Buzzard have made of the story of the 'Big Snake' which terrorised women at St Helen's, on the outskirts of Hastings, in the early autumn of 1934? The protagonists of this episode were a market gardener (not of Bulgarian extraction) called Jobson, a cemetery supervisor called Horridge, and a grave-digger who stated, after the snake had been seen wriggling down a large drain outside the cemetery, 'It was coiled three times round a tree trunk as big as my body, and it was as thick as my thigh. It was light brown, with black rings. I did not stop to see any more.' Let us not stop either, noting only, before we leave this primal scene, that the name of the grave-digger was Deeprose.

None of the following articles, bizarre though they may appear, have been altered in any way, beyond some standardization of spelling and punctuation, some occasional abridgement dictated by lack of space, and the shortening of some of the longer headlines. There was no room for the full story of the Big Snake of Hastings, nor will the reader find reports of Court proceedings, nor any of their favourite writers such as Mr Bernard Levin, who have already published selections of their best pieces. Nor unfortunately was there room for the long and extraordinary story of the Lost Books of Livy, which, following hotly on the discovery of the Bassano Archives forgery of the 1920s, rivals the more recent blunders over the Mussolini and Hitler Diaries. It would have been churlish, too, to have reprinted the article by a famous classical scholar in which, owing to a typing error, the word 'trash' is used throughout in place of 'past'. For as Mr Philip Howard points out on page 248 we all make mistakes, and as the chambermaid added, the little ones are often the worst. But let us pass over that (careful now, Printer) and on to the main feast. Take it with a glass of wine, or a bottle, but do not add salt, for *The Times* is a newspaper of record, and an authoritative source of news.

STEPHEN WINKWORTH

SMARTNESS: A STUDY IN SECRET SIN

When I first went to a war I objected to smartness for purely military reasons. I had to waste upon rubbing up my buttons precious hours that might have been spent in devising ways of outwitting the wiles of the Dutchman. In the present war my case is altered: in addition to the privilege of buying my own outfit and the bulk of my food, his Gracious Majesty allows me to pay a servant to clean my buttons. I say this by way of preface, so that if I have cause to cast reflections on military smartness you will know that I am not actuated by any selfish or personal motives. My whole case against smartness is that it introduces a widespread dishonesty into an otherwise straightforward profession.

This Great Betrayal came about at the time when Labour first became articulate, and struck blindly round at many cherished institutions. Why should the soldier be better dressed than the chimney-sweep or the dustman? Why should there be baths in barracks and not in Bermondsey? Such were the murmurs: and there were ugly whispers of 'gilded popinjays'. If the soldiers had gallantly stood their ground they would have won universal respect and support. A golden statue would have been a meet reward for the general who had stoutly answered, 'We are popinjays because we like to be popinjays. It is a man's duty to make the most of himself.' But there was no Horatius to hold the bridge: the soldiers sought refuge in subterfuges and mystification. Smartness was due to the exigencies of military service; it was woven deeply into the fabric of a fighting force; it had a tactical and strategical value.

That was how the saga started, and each successive bard has added his stanza. The thing grew amazingly. One fancies it must have astonished its parents. Anyhow, today every regular soldier implicitly believes that smartness was introduced deliberately into the Army with a sordid utilitarian purpose, and is prepared to maintain that it is the mainspring of every Christian, military, and other virtue. These virtues increase in proportion to the rank of the officer with whom you discuss them. The company commander modestly attributes to smartness his men's discipline, sobriety, bravery, cunning, truthfulness, and intensity of purpose; to these the colonel adds faith, hope, marksmanship, and charity; the brigadier adds chastity and quick recognition of targets; and so on through the whole military hierarchy.

Smartness in Orders

The truth comes to a newly-joined officer with startling suddenness as soon as he is passed off the square and begins to receive orders from his superiors. The importance of giving orders smartly on the public parade ground has already been dinned into him with some vehemence. He is told that he must not alter the wording in the slightest, or even pause in the wrong place; the men will at once notice anything incorrect, will consider he has not been properly educated in his profession, and will give his orders scant respect.

But his own orders come to him in writing, in the secrecy of his chamber, and he looks in vain for the smartness. They are ungrammatical and ill-spelled: words are used in a wholly unnatural sense and with the most awkward grammatical constructions. It does not matter where you go in the Army, this is the general rule.

If the adjutant of a Regular battalion came on parade with a single button unfastened a shudder would sweep over the whole parade ground. The same adjutant can put two split infinitives in his orders every night for a week, with an extra 'and which' on Sunday, and nobody will take the slightest notice. Yet the first is a momentary slip, while the second betrays a constant slovenly habit of mind.

The Army has a passion for numbers. About twice a week an officer is asked to make a return showing the number of certain men or articles 'in possession'. The orders always come in the same form:

Please send in return by 3.0 a.m. Friday showing number of uninoculated Wesleyans (or B.F. smoke helmets, or rounds of American ammunition) in your platoon. Nil returns must be rendered.

The first impulse of the ingenuous subaltern is to make a clean breast of it: speak the truth and shame the devil: add up all the Wesleyans, helmets, Chicago squibs, that he possesses, and share the secret with the adjutant. But then he reads again the last sentence. 'Must' is a strong word, especially when underlined. He must render a nil return. His not to reason why. Reluctantly forsaking all the lessons of his childhood, and feeling at the same time that his poor Wesleyans may be missing a good thing, he writes nil on a page of his notebook and 'renders' same . . .

Military Typewriting

Military typewriting is, of course, a thing to itself. The astonishing thing about it is not that it is always wrong, but that there is an extraordinary uniformity in its wrongdoing. 'Batallion' and 'acommodation' pursue you like spectres from Aldershot to Albert. One feels that there must be some method behind it all, some Hidden Hand to direct it.

When the war is over and I am an old man I mean to investigate it; and some day, somewhere – it may be up a marble stair in Whitehall, or in some oblong block of bricks at Chatham or Woolwich, or in a tin shanty on Salisbury Plain – I shall find the secret office of the Acting Deputy Assistant who really cuts the ice in the matter of Military Education, Typewriting Department. There, on the shelf beside him, I shall see, neatly bound in its smooth red cover, the Manual of Military Typewriting, that instructs the aspirant that 'principle' and 'principal' are alternative methods of spelling the same word; and that 'separate' must always have a third 'e' in its middle – 'seperate areas', 'seperated cases', 'seperation allowance'. Pinned on the wall is the famous General Routine Order ordering all Army typists to begin all words that they do not understand with capital letters – as a mark of respect, and the Schedule of the course of instruction that teaches men to split infinitives at the gallop, as cavalrymen split lemons. And in a special niche over the mantelpiece is a bust of that prince of Army typists who first invented the word 'mot', that keeps the reader wondering whether 'm' is a mistake for 'n' or a penultimate 's' has fallen out on the line of march; now most commonly used by all branches of the service in the phrase, 'It is mot necessary . . .'

In the middle of this Great War no patriot outside Parliament can afford to waste his energies in purely destructive criticism. As the Pope said when Galileo told him that the earth moved round the sun, 'That is all very well, but what are you going to do about it?'

5 February 1918

'. . . a special niche over the mantelpiece'
[MILITARY TYPEWRITING]

THE GREAT SEAL

The brief announcement, which appeared in *The Times* of yesterday, that Sir F. E. Smith had gone to Paris raises interesting questions relating to the custody of the Great Seal during the absence of the Lord Chancellor from this country. There are two fixed points in constitutional usage on this matter. It is indisputable that the Great Seal, the specific emblem of sovereignty, cannot be legally taken out of the kingdom. There is, further, no provision in the Constitution for the absence from the kingdom of the Lord Chancellor, as Lord Keeper of the Great Seal, except by the delegation of the duties of the office to a Commission.

It is understood that, while the Great Seal has been left in its accustomed place of security in this country, Commissioners have not been appointed for its care and custody during Sir F. E. Smith's absence. The new Lord Chancellor, it is stated, has only gone to Paris for a few days in order to hand over the legal bureau which he has formed there for the assistance of the British representatives to the Conference, to Sir Gordon Hewart, his successor as chief Law Officer. He is not engaged on any business connected with the office of Lord Chancellor, and it is considered unlikely that he will be called out of the country again. In any case, it was urged yesterday that, although the Great Seal was at home and the Lord Keeper abroad, they could be brought together in a few hours if any emergency should arise.

Still, constitutional lawyers were asking whether there had not been a departure from the practice of centuries. The only Lord Keeper who ever took the Great Seal out of the kingdom was Cardinal Wolsey, when on a mission to France for Henry VIII, in 1521. Even he, however, forbore to take it farther than Calais, which was then part of the English Dominions. It is believed that no other Lord Chancellor left the country to fulfil a public engagement until Lord Haldane visited America in the autumn of 1913 to deliver the annual address to the American Bar Association.

The position, however, was so well established by tradition that before Lord Haldane's departure it was announced that the King had appointed three Commissioners – Lord Morley of Blackburn, Lord Beauchamp, and Sir Herbert Cozens-Hardy, the Master of the Rolls – Commissioners for the care and custody of the Great Seal 'during any absence' of the then Lord Chancellor from the kingdom. Although Lord Haldane was away only just over a fortnight, it was held that this measure was demanded by constitutional propriety. The question was even asked whether the mere delivery up of the Great Seal by Lord Haldane had not determined his Chancellorship.

Lord Brougham's Holiday

That question was answered in the negative, and Lord Brougham's adventures with the Great Seal of William IV might have been cited in support. All the trouble which arose from his Scottish holiday in 1834 would have been averted if he had carried out his original intention of taking a trip up the Rhine. But Brougham found that he could not leave the kingdom without putting the Great Seal in Commission, at a cost to himself of £1,400. As he was not prepared for so expensive a holiday, he went to Scotland, taking the Great Seal with him. Great scandal was caused when the ladies at a country house at which Brougham was staying played a practical joke on him by removing the Great Seal from his bedroom and hiding it. When he recovered the precious object from a tea-chest in the drawing-room, he allowed the ladies to make pancakes with it by pouring the ingredients between the discs. But he never again became Lord Keeper of the Great Seal.

Only one Great Seal has been irrevocably lost. This was the first of George III, and it was stolen from Lord Thurlow's house in 1784. On the previous day Pitt had decided to appeal to the country, and, as the Whigs wished to avert a General Election, they were charged with the burglary. For a proclamation summoning or dissolving Parliament is not valid unless it bears the Great Seal. It is the instrument by which the will of the Sovereign is declared in other high matters, such as the grant of charters, the making of treaties, the issuing of patents of nobility, the furnishing of credentials to Ambassadors, and the appointment of Colonial Governors.

The Seal Buried by Lord Eldon

Eldon was so careful a custodian of the Great Seal that he always made sure that it was safe in his bedroom before retiring. One night in 1812 a fire occurred at his house. He rushed into the garden with the Great Seal in his arms, and buried it in a flower-bed. But, as Mr Michael MacDonagh recalls in one of his books on Parliament: Eldon was, by his own confession, 'so enchanted with the pretty sight of the maids, who had turned out of their beds and were handing in buckets of water to the fire-engine in their shifts', and 'so alarmed for the safety of Lady Eldon', that he quite forgot where he had buried the Great Seal. 'You never saw anything so ridiculous,' he said, 'as seeing the whole family down the walks dibbling with bits of sticks until we found it.'

If the career of the Great Seal is less adventurous than of old, it is because modern Lord Chancellors have scrupulously respected its traditions.

22 January 1919

MEN'S HATS LARGER: A CURIOUS RESULT OF THE WAR

Are men's heads growing larger? This is a question which manufacturers of hats are asking just now, for the orders which are coming through at present reveal a marked increase in sizes. The standard sizes formerly were $6\frac{1}{2}$, $6\frac{5}{8}$, $6\frac{7}{8}$, but now these are by no means popular. Instead, the majority of hats are made in sizes from $6\frac{5}{8}$ to $7\frac{1}{8}$.

A man wearing a hat over size 7 used to be credited with a superabundance of brains, and if a hatter was asked to get a friend a size $7\frac{1}{8}$ hat he usually had plenty of banter or flattery ready, suited to the customer's taste.

'. . . the pretty sight of the maids'
[THE GREAT SEAL]

Manufacturers are inclined to the belief that it is a result of the war. One manufacturer said that pathologists he had consulted were of opinion that the incessant gunfire on the Western front had caused men's heads to increase a little in size, and it had been proved that men suffering from shell shock after leaving hospital could not wear the cap they had before they were stricken down.

13 May 1919

AN ADMIRER'S GIFT

Miss Lillian Russell, the popular comedy star, was the recipient yesterday of one of the most valuable of many presents she has received during her stage career. She was standing on the steps of her hotel at Atlantic City when a friend came up and introduced a grey-haired man accompanying him.

The grey-haired man, whose name is Schuyler, told Miss Russell he had been an admirer of her art for many years, and would like to show his appreciation by making her a little gift.

'It is worth £2,400,' he added. 'That will be lovely,' replied Miss Russell, graciously.

'I think you'll like it,' said Mr Schuyler: 'it is the most beautiful and costly article in my establishment, and I am real proud of it. My desire is that it should go to one whose artistic temperament will recognize fine craftsmanship,' with much more to the same effect.

'Please tell me what it is,' begged Miss Russell, all happy expectation.

'It's a gold trimmed coffin,' replied Mr Schuyler, who is Philadelphia's leading undertaker.

29 August 1919

MR 'PUSSYFOOT' CAPTURED AND PARADED

Mr 'Pussyfoot' Johnson, the prohibition advocate who has come over from America to aid a campaign in this country, was to have engaged in debate in Essex Hall, Strand, yesterday afternoon, with Mr Marshall Banks, of the Anti-Prohibition League, but the hall was rushed by medical students, who captured the visitor and made him the victim of an extraordinary 'rag'. He was taken to King's College first and then escorted by a large band of the hilarious students to the West End, where he was eventually released by the police near Oxford Circus.

The meeting was organized by the Central Committee of the Overseas Club and Patriotic League to give the public an opportunity to hear both sides of the prohibition question. Mr F. A. McKenzie, recently returned from a tour in the United States, was to preside. The back of the hall was packed with students, who maintained a fire of lively interruptions, heedless of appeals for fair play to both sides.

One of the opposition was allowed to speak from the platform, and said that it was for Britishers to decide whether they should be wet or dry; they wanted no advice or ornate speeches from the States and the sooner Mr Johnson realized that the better. (Cheers.)

Mr Johnson, in a brief lull, tried to open the debate. He agreed, he said, that it was 'up to' the British people to decide the question without the intervention of Americans or anyone else, but he came to this country at the invitation, and partly at the expense, of British people, and he claimed the right to speak when invited to do so.

The interruptions increased, and many joined in singing:

Old soldiers never die,
They only fade away.

The uproar in the hall and in the street outside increased, and after a struggle a fresh body of students entered the hall and rushed the platform. Bags of white flour were thrown, one bursting on 'Pussyfoot', who was seized and carried out of the hall.

A Commandeered Van

The students had laid their plans well. To prevent any possibility of 'Pussyfoot's' escape, pickets entirely surrounded the hall and parties of students held the steps which lead from Essex Street to the Embankment. On leaving the hall the 'raiding party' was joined by hundreds of students, and 'Pussyfoot' was carried shoulder high along the Strand. When the premises of Messrs W.H. Smith and Sons were reached an empty delivery van was commandeered, the horse unyoked, and 'Pussyfoot' was placed on the vehicle, which was then drawn by a boisterous party along the Strand and into the quadrangle of King's College. Mr Johnson was carried up to the balcony and requested to speak, but could not make himself heard above the din. Then followed what the students described as a 'christening' scene. A bottle of Bass was emptied over 'Pussyfoot', while the crowd shouted themselves hoarse.

The procession was re-formed in the quadrangle, and went along the Strand to Trafalgar Square, headed by a tin trumpet 'band'. There were many banners in the procession. One bore the following lines:

> Mr Pussyfoot, miaow-wow:
> Mr Pussyfoot, miaow-wow!
> Fancy coming from America to try
> To make Old England dry!
> Uncle Sam stood it like a lamb,
> But if you think we are going to allow
> Any crank of a Yank to put us on the water tank –
> Mr Pussyfoot, miaow-wow!

Procession to West End

At Trafalgar Square, instead of holding a demonstration, as had been intended, the processionists turned up

Charing Cross Road and went by way of Leicester Square to Piccadilly Circus.

By the time Piccadilly Circus was reached, 'Pussyfoot' had been transferred from the cart to the shoulders of the students. At the head of the procession was a banner, looking very like a lantern screen from a college lecture room. It bore the inscription, in coloured chalks, 'Pussyfoot, Miaow!' and underneath, side by side, rough drawings of a cat and a foaming flagon of beer.

Behind the banner, smiling and bowing to left and right, came 'Pussyfoot' himself, high over the heads of the demonstrators. Then came a battalion of students, marching in fours, and escorted by policemen, who seemed to be enjoying the fun. The marching song was, 'We've got Pussyfoot', repeated ad lib; with occasional variations, as 'Who've we got? Pussyfoot, Pussyfoot, Pussyfoot!' Many of the students showed signs of the scrimmage through which they had gone. One out of every three had his shoulders whitened with flour. Some had lost hats and caps. At least one had a well-developed 'black eye'.

By the time Oxford Circus was reached a large body of police had arrived. The procession turned into Great Portland Street, and here the police decided to take action. After a scrimmage which lasted about ten minutes the police succeeded in rescuing 'Pussyfoot'. A military motor-car was commandeered to convey Mr Johnson to his rooms, and shortly afterwards the students dispersed.

One of the leaders of the students informed a representative of *The Times* that there is a feeling among them that London does not know that it is a 'Varsity' town. 'We think,' he said, 'that a "Varsity rag" now and then will show the country that we are alive.' The 'rag' was prearranged, a telephone message being circulated to the various hospitals late yesterday forenoon that 'the meeting was to take place at King's College'. One of the students said that 'Pussyfoot' at first 'showed fight', but afterwards took it very calmly and pulled out some cigarettes. Everybody started shouting, 'Pussyfoot's smoking.'

14 November 1919

WIFE KILLED IN A DREAM

Mr James Sapienza, president of the Cement Manufacturing Company, Irvington, New Jersey, killed his wife in a dream yesterday night. He dreamed that his daughter, who was sleeping in the same room, was being attacked by assassins, and he fired on them, with the result that he killed his wife.

According to Mr Sapienza's story, for some time past he had been receiving letters demanding money, accompanied by threats of death if he failed to pay. He gave the letters, which he believed came from the 'Black Hand' gang, to the police, but the threats got on his nerves to such an extent that he obtained a licence to carry a revolver, and always slept with it under his pillow. The neighbours said that he had become a nervous wreck in consequence of worrying over the letters.

Yesterday night Mr Sapienza, his wife, and their two-year-old daughter went to bed as usual about 10. Towards midnight Mr Sapienza thought he heard the window open. Turning over, he saw two masked men enter the room, armed with knives. One went and stood over the daughter, with his arm raised to strike. In frantic terror Mr Sapienza fired the pistol which he was clutching in his hand beneath the pillow. He heard the report, and then found himself sitting up in bed. The room was empty and quiet, and there was no window open. The terrified man heard a moan from his wife. Switching on the light he saw blood trickling from a wound in her head. He then realized he had been dreaming. But his wife was dead. The bullet had gone through the pillow clean through her head.

After reading the letters handed by Mr Sapienza to the police, and hearing the testimony of the neighbours as to his condition, the magistrate said he believed his story, and released him on bail. The unfortunate man, who stated that he was deeply attached to his wife, is completely prostrated.

27 November 1919

'THE JELLOUS GOVERNESS'

A large audience assembled yesterday in the Æolian Hall to see Miss Daisy Ashford, and hear her read extracts from her famous book, *The Young Visiters*. The matinee was in aid of the Catholic Stage Guild, and was delightfully informal. There was no programme, but music was promised as well as the readings. A charming young lady played a violin solo before the chair was taken by Mr Hilaire Belloc, but afterwards the promise of more music was quite forgotten, for the audience were told they might ask Miss Ashford questions, and also that they were going to hear her sister Angela's book, *The Jellous Governess*.

The Jellous Governess was read from MS. by Miss Ida Molesworth, who enjoyed it as much as her audience. It was written at the age of eight by Angela Ashford, who is now married and living in Southampton. For the age of the child that wrote it, it was an even more extraordinary effort than *The Young Visiters*. When the tale opens Mr and Mrs Holes are sitting at the fire, he reading the paper, she the *Strand Magazine*. She says she wants a baby. 'Elizabeth,' says the husband, 'it is the one thing I've been wishing. I would like to adopt one.' Mrs Holes declares a preference for one of her own. Later 'the doctor's bold step was heard at the door'. He has a cardboard box tied up. 'I hear you've been wishing a baby,' he says. 'Is it a boy or a girl?' Mrs Holes asked. 'I don't know,' says the doctor. He lays the box on the eider down and going away 'slammed the door with his feet because he was holding his top hat with both hands'. Mrs Holes says, 'What a dear little fat baby', and 'What a pity it has not got its eyes open. Hadn't we better put something on it?' and having secured the blue shawl she had when a baby herself, 'skips back to bed'. Mr Holes buttons the last button of his waistcoat and hurries to his office.

Six months later Mr Holes, who 'smoked to a low degree, being rather a Cockney man', decides they should have a governess for the child. Mrs Holes points out that baby is too young, but he thinks that it is not too soon for

'. . . his top hat with both hands'
[THE JELLOUS GOVERNESS]

the baby to get used to its future teacher. So he dresses in his best to go to town to look for one, and comes down 'looking like a duke and not a mere mister'; he tells his wife he has put on his best black suit, 'a clean shirt, and a pair of scarlet socks with a hole, but it doesn't show'. As there was a button off his trousers, one leg was shorter than the other.

The search for the governess was very amusing. Dismissing certain ladies whose services were offered from their choice (one had 'boisterous feet' and was 'cow-like'), Mrs Holes, who smacks her lips at breakfast over the thought of a dinner in town, goes up finally to choose the lady. She dined off rabbit and meringues, and drank sherry wine and went 'into the depths of London' to do her shopping.

Miss Junick (it sounded like Junick) was the chosen governess. When asked her salary she said, 'Either five pounds or fourteen pounds, but I don't do much for five.'

The tragedy of the 'jellous governess' begins from the moment she arrives. She wants a baby of her own, and decides to go out at once and see the doctor. But Mrs Holes may ask why she wants to go out, so she says, 'To buy some Beecham's pills.' She asks the doctor 'Could you get me a baby?' 'Well,' he says, 'the question is are you married?' Miss Junick says no, so the doctor is sorry, but can do nothing. 'I would marry you myself, but I have a wife.' Miss Junick brightens up, and decides on a bold course. 'I wasn't thinking what I was saying,' she said: 'I am married,' so the doctor sent a page boy next day with a baby. This chapter is headed 'The Private Arrival of Miss Junick's Baby'.

Unfortunately, Miss Junick does not like the baby which proves to be ugly, and she is very angry to find a bill for £1 in the box. She throws the baby away and decides to steal Mrs Holes's child when it is two years old. Mrs Holes dies of grief and Mr Holes 'loses his hair and seldom brushes what remains', his nose 'became red and large', and he sits by the empty grate saying, 'Would I had Miss Junick by the scruff of the neck.' One day a young man rushes in.

'Father, don't you know me?' 'I am very glad to see you back, my son,' Mr Holes says, and the tragedy ends on a joyous note.

The hall was full of chuckles through the reading, and a clergyman, proposing a vote of thanks, said he belonged to a dreary commission dealing with the decline of the birth-rate. He thought they would do infinitely better if they would stop sitting and adopt *The Jellous Governess* as a pamphlet.

6 December 1919

A LION AT THE FEAST

PARIS Marguery's restaurant, which is still famous, despite the trend of fashion westwards, entertained yesterday some thirty theatrical and circus stars in quest of something new to eat.

The *pièce de resistance* was the back of the four-year-old lion Mascotte, which Marcel, the tamer, purchased last year for 6,000 francs. Mascotte recently met with an accident and had to be shot. Needless to say that in these hard times roast lion is not to be disdained. At the head of the diners was the actress Mistinguette. An interested spectator was Mascotte's year-old son, Adolphe, on the look-out for tit-bits. Truth requires it to be said that lion flesh was voted by the company to be somewhat tasteless unless well sauced.

5 April 1920

WHISKY BY TORPEDO

NEW YORK In direct contradiction to the statements persistently circulated by the Anti-Saloon League, Dr M. S. Gregory, Director of Bellevue Hospital, reports today that the number of patients suffering from over-indulgence in alcohol is daily increasing.

The report forms the basis of a public attack upon the Federal authorities responsible for the enforcement of prohibition by Mr Bird S. Coler, Commissioner of Public Welfare. Mr Coler declares that the best citizens boast of evading the law, and says that owing to the laxity of the authorities liquor is everywhere obtainable.

The extent to which smuggling has developed is illustrated by a report from Detroit describing how electrically operated torpedoes loaded with whisky are being sent daily across the Detroit River from the Canadian to the American shore. The torpedoes submerge 100 ft and take five minutes to cross the river. They are emptied on the American side, ballasted with water, and sent back to Canada for reloading.

10 May 1920

COMMANDER OF THE PIRATES

Ernest Hargreaves, aged 16, of Shadwell, who described himself as 'Commander of the Pirates and President of Libertia', announced that he was sick of life as lived as present, and declared 'So now starts my career of piracy with modern weapons. I will terrorise the world' was sent to prison for one month at Leeds yesterday for the theft of a bicycle.

24 August 1920

OUTCRY CAUSED BY INVENTOR

NEW YORK Thomas Edison, the famous inventor, has brought a hornet's nest about his ears by a scathing condemnation of the intelligence and knowledge of American university men which he delivered after studying the examination papers of 300 applicants for positions in the Edison factory.

The papers, which were drawn up by Mr Edison himself, contained 141 questions, which the unsuccessful candidates and leading educators denounce as 'silly'. The following are specimens:

> Who wrote 'Home, Sweet Home'?
> Where is Kenosha?
> What is the greatest depth of the Atlantic Ocean?
> What country consumed most tea before the war?

Two hundred and seventy out of 300 candidates succeeded in passing this test, upon which Mr Edison recorded his disgust at their imperfection.

The New York Globe yesterday dispatched a representative to Mr Edison's house in order to seek an interview. The representative pressed Mr Edison's electric bell. It would not work.

13 May 1921

RAIN BY CONTRACT

TORONTO A 'rainmaker' named Hatfield is under a contract with the farmers of Alberta to increase the rainfall in the dry sections of the country.

Hatfield is established in a small hut at the lonely margin of Chappice Lake, 20 miles from Medicine Hat. He expresses absolute confidence that he can fulfil the contract. He says: 'The average rainfall in this district during the past four years is below 2 in. I am bound by contract to increase that to four. Actually, I hope to make it nearer 8 in. As to my ability, you may judge at the end of July, when the contract expires.'

All the morning on which Hatfield had this interview with the Toronto Globe correspondent rain was steadily falling. Since the interview 24 hours have elapsed and rain is still falling. Hatfield began work on Sunday 1 May and promised the first rain in six days. Rain began on the third day and has continued with brief interruptions ever since. It is five years since this dry area has known such a steady seasonal rainfall.

Hatfield is from California, and the contract, for a period of three months, is to produce rain over a territory with a radius of 100 miles. Nature is to be given credit for half the rainfall, light or heavy, and the rain-maker credit for the remainder. He gets $4,000 (£1,000) for each inch of rainfall beyond the 2 in. normal, with a maximum reward of $8,000 (£2,000) whatever the results. The contract is a legal document and is in safety in a deposit box at Medicine Hat.

As a final evidence of human faith or credulity the $8,000 have been secured by voluntary subscriptions from the heads of families in the area of the rain-maker's operations.

16 May 1921

[After some anxious weeks Hatfield's contract was fulfilled following a four-hour rainstorm in July. Psychic rather than physical methods appear to have been employed to produce this remarkable result. Further details of rain-making techniques are given in a report from Bulawayo in 1928. In this African version victims are first strangled with grass ropes, then placed in a pot, boiled and thrown in a river.]

ANYTHING FOR A QUIET LIFE

A New York couple, who by mutual agreement have not spoken to each other for nine years, although continuing to live together, yesterday, on the expiration of their pact, renewed it for another nine years. The couple are Mr and Mrs Charles Baumann. The husband, who is a tapestry artist, is aged 75 and his wife 45. Describing the reasons for their silence Mr Baumann said:

'Nine years ago we found that we could not get on together owing to the great difference in our ages. We did not think alike on any subject so we agreed to disagree. We live in the same flat, but I rarely see my wife as she comes and goes as she pleases.'

Under the agreement Mr Baumann renounces all control over his children. He explained: 'My wife is relieved of all responsibility towards me, and I to her. Under our agreement she must support herself and three children. I take care of myself. Three of my own sons contribute to her support.'

Mr Baumann's first wife died in 1890 and by his two wives he has had seven boys and five girls.

20 July 1921

COCKTAILS FOR THE ELECT

The mixing of cocktails and the drinking of them is in a more advanced stage in Liverpool than in any other town in England which I have visited since the war. The moment the bars are opened in Liverpool, so also at that very moment do the cocktail drinkers seize their own special cocktails, sometimes in one hand and sometimes, I am afraid, in two, and drink them down.

From that moment until the bar closes expert mixers in the white robes of their office mix and shake and shake and mix until the bar is closed by the order of 'DORA'.

Let it be admitted at once that I have never anywhere in

this country drank such tantalising cocktails, so difficult of analysis or momentarily so pleasing to the palate, as I drank in the Exchange and Adelphi hotels in Liverpool last week. I knew the names of some of those which I tasted, but there were others, very insidious, cloudy and beautiful, which had no name, and each of which could be made by only one man in Liverpool – perhaps indeed, in the world. Those who desired those special drinks had to go to the one mixer who alone knew the secret of them.

Not one of the many mixers that I saw had a small following. Each had many customers. Each took an obvious delight in the mysterious and secret rites of his office, and each, I think, made a nice income out of the special rewards which delighted people gave to him.

At some of the bars other drinks are drunk, but at some I saw only cocktails consumed. I cannot say how many cocktails were drunk by each customer nor how many cherries were spitefully skewered on a stick, but I never saw a man who had a single cocktail and then went away. At the same time I never saw a man in Liverpool who was any worse for drinking cocktails, which appeared only to make them very happy, not only with themselves but also with complete strangers.

The fact that business is very bad in Liverpool may account for the popularity of the cocktail, which no doubt also owes much of its popularity there to the coming and going of American visitors. But they were not by any means all Americans whom I saw in the bars at Liverpool. I am not an American myself.

Cocktails as made in Liverpool are certainly seductive, and man is always weak. I was, and three days in Liverpool drinking cocktails did not improve my appetite nor my health. There have been complaints about my liver ever since I returned to London. The hospitality of Liverpool people is, however, proverbial.

25 July 1921

[DORA – Defence of the Realm Act (1914). In Amendment No. 3 (1915) a Central Control Board was established to monitor sales of liquor – insobriety in the services, not to mention among civilian workers in armament factories, being regarded as too obvious a peril to national security. The present pub licensing hours in the United Kingdom have their origins in this act.]

'CHARLIE' CHAPLIN'S SCHOOLDAYS

'Charlie' Chaplin, as was stated in a telegram from our New York correspondent, published in *The Times* yesterday, states that he believes he went to school 'somewhere in Kennington', and that when he comes to England he will try to find the school if it still exists.

Mr T. A. Murch, headmaster of St Agnes's Church School, Kennington Park, in conversation with a representative of *The Times* yesterday, said that, though he has never seen the comedian in a film, and until yesterday had never been interested in Chaplin the man, he is satisfied from recent statements by the comedian himself, from the school records, and from his own vivid memories, that 'Charlie' Chaplin and a certain 'curious boy' he knew between the years 1904 and 1909 are one and the same.

An old register of St Agnes's School reads as follows:

'Chaplin, Charles, son of Chaplin, Charles of 191 East Street (Walworth) admitted from the Michael Faraday School, left 26.6.09. Address (during the later years of his school life), 31, Myatt Road (Camberwell).'

'It is quite in keeping with the character of Master Chaplin, as I knew him,' said Mr Murch, 'that he should not remember the name of his school. I have heard, too, that he is not at all sure of his age. I last saw him when he was perhaps 16 years old, in Brixton Road, a somewhat ludicrous little figure, I thought, with his hands covered with cotton gloves much too long in the fingers. He spoke of his desire to go on the stage, and I was amused, because I had in mind only the legitimate stage.'

At school, according to Mr Murch, 'Charlie' was a

dreamer, rather irresponsible. His general conduct was fairly satisfactory, for Mr Murch cannot find any black marks against him, except for unpunctuality. This was his besetting sin. He was late about three times a week, though his excuses and his manner of making them were so plausible that to punish him was usually out of the question. He used to shuffle along in a queer way, with head held slightly to one side, and his eyes furtively looking upward, to see if the master was watching. He was a great mimic, and a source of endless amusement to his fellow pupils in his varied antics, both in and out of school.

1 September 1921

[Chaplin's reply was received a few days later from New York. He was very interested, he stated, to read of his namesake's wonderful ability and genius for pranks. 'I am afraid, though, it wasn't me.' On 19 June 1909 Chaplin was 20 years old. He left school at 10.]

ABSENT-MINDED

The most absent-minded man in Germany has been discovered at the big railway junction of Kreiensen, in Brunswick, where he discovered that he had left his pocket-book containing over 800 marks (25 shillings) at the ticket office of his starting point.

As he had not a copper in his pocket the booking clerk lent him the money to telegraph about it, and the reply came that his pocket-book had been found, so he borrowed some more money to buy the ticket to go back and get his lost property. He set off, and returned to the junction looking delighted that he had found his money, but then discovered that he had left behind a box containing sausages, bread, and shirts. Just as he was explaining to a sympathetic booking clerk that he had had a second run of ill-luck he dropped 500 marks (15s 3d) which a girl noticed, picked up and gave to him. He thanked her at such length that the train which was to take him farther on went off without him and he was forced to confess that he had left his umbrella in the rack.

22 October 1921

A PALACE FOR TITANIA

'Titania's Palace', an exquisite example of miniature house construction, decoration, and furnishing, is being made by its designer, Major Sir Nevile Wilkinson, Ulster King of Arms and Registrar of the Order of St Patrick – well known also as a designer and etcher of book-plates – at his studio in Duchess Street, Portland Place. He has given years of thought and work to the scheme, and when it is completed it promises to be a stately and magnificent mansion, worthy, in its enchanting diminutiveness, of the fairy land of imagination.

The Palace will cover 60 square feet, and some of its two-storied sections will rise to a height of 3 ft and over. By means of glass panels complete views of the interiors are afforded. The entrance hall to this home of Titania and Oberon – as we know them in *A Midsummer Night's Dream* – has been completed. The floor is composed of tiny marble squares, black and white, which have been cut and polished at Torquay. Panels of Connemara marble, misty green in hue, line the lower parts of the walls. Then there are pieces of tapestry worked in colours, each showing a fairy maiden holding a shield of arms and framed in golden mosaic. The ceiling consists of 12 recesses, bordered with gilded shells picked up on the shores of Brittany, and in each recess is painted the coat of arms of some famous Florentine family, one being that of Alighieri, of which Dante was a member. At the far end of the hall is a raised platform of inlaid woods leading to silver gates, which give admission to those parts of the palace that are still to be made and furnished – the Throne Room, the Hall of the Fairy Kiss, the Chapel, Oberon's study, and the boudoir and bedroom of Titania. The paintings, tapestries, and mosaics, with which the hall is so richly decorated are, despite their tiny proportions, finished with the utmost care and artistic taste.

10 December 1921

[Sir Nevile Wilkinson also wrote a book, *Yvette in Italy*, in which the story of Titania's Palace is told. It appears that he was inspired to carry out the work by Titania herself. The fairy method of locomotion, he explained in a lecture, is 'flashing'. One day Titania, before going out for a 'flash', came to Sir Nevile and told him that children were losing their interest in fairies. It was his duty to do something about this. So he wrote the book, and took up 'tinycraft'. Nowadays, he concluded, to encourage him in the good work, the Queen of the Fairies kept flashing to him all the time.

Sir Nevile, before he developed his interest in fairies, was on the march to Bloemfontein and served on the staff of the Mediterranean Expeditionary Force during the 1914–18 War. He was knighted in 1920.

Titania's Palace was sold in 1978 to Legoland, a theme park in Denmark.]

BURGLARS' UNIVERSITY

A diploma issued by a training school for burglars was found by the police among the effects of Joseph Lauzon, a well-known cracksman, who was arrested at Washington yesterday. The institution, which is situated at Los Angeles, names itself 'The Wayne Strong School of Safe-work'.

Its diploma certifies that 'Mr Joseph Lauzon has been a student at this school of safework and that he has satisfactorily completed the subjects mentioned herein as

taught by our safe experts. He is hereby awarded a diploma as an acknowledgement of his proficiency and in recognition of his accomplishments.' The list of subjects referred to consists of 'safe-opening, combination-setting, safe-repairing, and safe-lock work'.

Lauzon's last piece of work brought him in loot to the value of £40,000. Many of his former classmates at the safecracking school, he told the police, are reaping a golden harvest in New York and other large cities.

4 May 1922

A SILENT WIFE

A Chicago Judge today granted a divorce to Mr William Walter Raleigh on the grounds of his wife's silence.

The plaintiff informed the Court that, although his wife lived in his house, she had not spoken to him for eighteen years. 'It has been like living with a ghost,' he said. He had consulted physicians in the effort to get her to talk, but it was impossible to surprise her into uttering a word.

7 October 1922

SCHOOLBOY HOWLERS

The annual 'howler' competition of the *University Correspondent* has again produced a joyous collection of schoolboy mistakes contributed by their masters and mistresses. The translations of Smith minor from the dead languages are always fruitful. *De mortuis nil nisi bonum* produces on this occasion as an English version, 'There's nothing but bones in the dead'; and *Ne plus ultra*, 'There's nothing beyond Ulster'. *Tertium quid* 'is a legal term meaning six shillings and eightpence'.

There are some excellent examples of miscellaneous 'information'. 'A grass widow,' we are told, 'is the wife of a dead vegetarian.' The author of 'Britain has a temporary climate' was evidently a youthful cynic, and one suspects the same hand in the definition of 'ambiguity' as 'telling the truth when you don't mean to'. Other specimens are:

Palsy is a kind of new writer's dance.

Letters in sloping print are hysterics.

Etiquette is the noise you make when you sneeze.

In the departments of history, geography, grammar, and literature the following occur:

The capital of Norway is Christianity.

No one has yet succeeded in edifying the dark lady of the sonnets.

The French Revolution was won violently, not by 'freedom slowly broadening down from President to President', as Tennyson wrote.

Guy's Hospital was built to commemorate the Gunpowder Plot.

Oceania is that continent which contains no land.
Mephistopheles was a Greek comic poet.

A mathematical problem is swept out of the way with a broad gesture in the definition, 'Things which are equal to the same thing are equal to anything else.' An expert in child psychology is required to explain the tortuousness of 'One of the chief uses of water is to save people from drowning in', and 'A circle is a rounded figure made up of a crooked straight line bent so as the ends meet.' There is, however, a simple directness about 'The plural of forget-me-not is forget-us-not.'

3 January 1923

[Some gems from subsequent years, recorded in the same publication, include 'Marriage, or the State of Holy Acrimony', and the triple definition: 'Evolution is what Darwin did; Revolution is a form of government abroad; Devolution is something to do with Satan.']

A DANGER OF RICHES

BERLIN A young Berlin bank clerk appeared in the Moabit Police Court today on the charge of assaulting a Berlin jeweller in a cafe in the Friedrichstrasse. According to the jeweller, the young man gave him a tremendous smack in the face for no apparent reason. The young bank clerk admitted that the reason could hardly be a good one.

'I hardly know myself why I struck him,' he replied to the Judge, 'except that I didn't like his face. I was sitting beside him when a blind beggar came in and begged from him, and there he sat, with his fat red face opposite an enormous portion of roast beef, with rings on his hand, and a grand suit, and his face a smug picture of avarice and humility. I said to myself, "He must give the beggar something. He simply must. He is rich; he is eating himself dazed, and he will never miss it." And when he replied, "On principle I give only to charitable societies," I was overcome by an unconquerable impulse. Something lifted my hand, and then the next thing I heard was the resounding smack on his perspiring cheeks.'

The Court found that the young man had acted under the influence of hysteria and inflicted a fine.

5 May 1923

ICE

All men, when the temperature is high, have their peculiar consolations. Being unable to discover cold in their physical surroundings, they imagine cold things after their own hearts. If their eye falls upon a map of the world, they look instinctively away from the equator towards the regions of chilly names. There, in the far north or south, they linger, and conjure up for themselves frozen dreams. They see before them wide fields of snow, they hear their imagined footsteps crunch in the powdered glitter; they, who are not explorers and in all their lives have ventured little abroad, behold the shining track of sledge-runners and feel the air plunge like knives between their fingers. They return, too, to their childhood – to the days when they would step aside to make splinters of a frozen puddle, or would send a stone, complaining like a curlew's call, across the glassy surface of a pond. They remember joyfully how they would trace the flowers and ferns that night had patterned on the nursery panes; how, in the garden, they would chip the hanging icicles from a window-sill and with what a tinkling they fell; how, when they went into open country, 'the withdrawn and tense sky', as Thoreau said, was 'groined like the aisles of a cathedral', and the polished air sparkled as if 'there were crystals of ice floating in it'.

For the power of ice, like all power, lies in imagination rather than in fact. Wayfarers gaze at a cube that is being delivered in the streets; it exercises a fascination over them

– a little, perhaps, because there is a sensible back-wash of cold as it passes, but chiefly for the sake of the vaster coolnesses that it suggests. As if in a Scandinavian fairy-story, the ice-merchant's jaded pony is transformed into a reindeer and its brazen harness into the northern bells. Through the opened door of the ice-van the watchers see, not ice merely, but a continent of Arctic wonders. For an instant they forget the sun, and the pavement, and the blistered paint; they are travellers among the massed glitter of innumerable frozen crystals, and they feel the wind of the snow plains swirl across their throats. So it is with the sound of ice. Itself no more than a chink of two sixpences, it is so powerful in its suggestion that the very air seems cleared by its ring on a silver spoon or by the soft chatter of its floating. Hearing or seeing or touching it, we receive in our minds a greater coolness than it can give to our bodies. We discover suddenly, as we discover each hot summer, that the English are ill-equipped with counters to great heat. Our streets are broad and naked of the perpetual half-shade of Italy; our windows are without shutters to admit the breeze and exclude the sun; our clothes, and the conventions that hold us to their stiffer detail, are not made for the dog-days. Ice is our single expedient. Because it stands alone and is rare, our imagination runs riot at the sight and thought of it. It leads us to the ends of the world and to the top of the nursery stair. When we were small it was a plaything if we could obtain or discover it. It lent its peculiar glamour of remoteness to some of the earliest stories we read, and now, because a heat-wave is upon us, we return to it with something more than physical eagerness – with a knowledge that there is romance in every association of it and a coolness in the stark simplicity of its name.

16 July 1923

[Written during a heatwave.]

AN ELEPHANT AND WIRELESS

When an elephant obeys its keeper, does it respond to voice only, or to the conjunction of voice and gesture? Does a wireless 'loud speaker' convey the tones of the voice sufficiently clearly to enter the consciousness of the elephant? Experiments devised to throw light on these two questions were tried at the Zoological Gardens yesterday evening in the presence of the Gardens staff, several representatives of the Press, and a large crowd of interested visitors.

The Marconi Company, at the instance of Mr L. G. Mainland, placed a powerful wireless receiver with a Marconiphone 'loud speaker' against the railing separating the two divisions of the paddock outside the elephant house. At the broadcasting station several miles away Said Ali, the Indian mahout, who has been at the Gardens in charge of the large female Indian elephant 'Indarini' last season and this season, was ready to give, at appointed intervals, four orders which the elephant is accustomed to obey. 'Indarini' was led to a spot just in front of the loud speaker, and stood there docilely munching potatoes and carib beans, while the experiments were explained on the wireless by Mr Mainland. Then came the first order to lie down. The individual intonations, first of Mr Mainland and then of Said Ali, could be recognized with the greatest ease, and the speaker was so clear that the visitors outside the railings heard distinctly. But the elephant took no notice. The second order, to get up, was plainly futile, as the first had not been obeyed. The third order was to salute, which the elephant is accustomed to do by raising its ears and trunk and trumpeting loudly. When the order came through 'Indarini' happened to have her head only a few feet from the loud speaker, and for a fraction of a second it seemed as if she were going to obey. The last order was to perform a favourite trick – to pick up coins thrown down in front of her. Here, again, she took no notice, simply ascertaining that the coins were not food, and then neglecting them.

Immediately after her failure to obey the wireless messages she was put through the orders, in succession, by one of the English keepers, and obeyed them with little reluctance, although she is much more docile with Said Ali than with an English keeper. So far as these experiments go, therefore, it would appear either that an elephant requires gesture as well as voice, or that the intonation of the loud speaker, clear enough to human beings, is insufficient for the animal's hearing.

10 August 1923

M. RAVEL IN LONDON

M. Maurice Ravel gave a concert of his own music at the Queen's Hall yesterday, which was not as well attended as it might have been, though small numbers were made up for by enthusiasm. M. Ravel's charm is something elfish and inscrutable. He draws his own portrait to begin with on the cover of his programme – a face with no illusions in it, no dreams of nonsense, practical in every line. Then he writes the words of his own song 'Nicolette' – firm, brief, and pointed. Then he conducts with a wrist as steady and supple and with as much economy of unnecessary motions as a man might practise with his razor. Lastly, he plays the piano in the low-pitched tone of ordinary conversation, as if he were merely telling you the common sense of the matter.

Besides all this he writes music, and is thought to have made some fame with it. It is no music of the passions; it yearns after no infinite; it takes a simple delight in the curious variety of things and the whimsicalities of persons on this good brown earth, as an interested spectator, not as a mænad or a moralist. It is grotesquely detached and vividly true.

The quartet, that startling proem to the twentieth century, tinkled and sparkled in that large hall. *Sostenuto* passages like the first movement asserted themselves nobly, *pizzicato* passages like the scherzo could still be heard with the mind's ear. The septet had more body; Miss Gwendolen Mason's harp cadenza was a remarkable performance. One could not find very much to say for M. Victor Brault's voice; he seemed to feel it a strain to get some of the notes. But one would not have missed that beautiful diction for worlds, and one does not often hear such thorough understanding of poet and composer. The 'Jeux d'eau' and the 'Sonatine' are always with us, it is true, but M. Pol-Morin managed, with his responsive Erard, to set them in a new light.

M. Ravel gives his second concert at the Æolian Hall on 16 January, when a new violin sonata will be played.

19 October 1923

A MILLION LISTENERS: THE FIRST YEAR OF BROADCASTING

Today is the first anniversary of the official beginning of broadcasting in this country. Remarkable developments have been seen since, on 14 November 1922, news bulletins and weather reports were sent out from wireless stations in London and Manchester, to be picked up by the few thousands of people who then possessed receiving sets, and it is estimated that at the present time approximately a million people in Great Britain listen on any night of the week to the programmes transmitted by the British Broadcasting Company. The Postmaster-General announced last week that 492,000 broadcasting licences had now been issued, and it may be taken that the majority of the licence-holders use more than one pair of telephones, and that many have added a loud speaker to their apparatus.

Two years ago English broadcasting was limited to a few amateurs who exchanged experimental messages among themselves. When officially regulated transmission was initiated the pioneers had to move cautiously and laboriously towards the considerable measure of success already achieved. The experience of America, where the existence of hundreds of competitive broadcasting stations had made for confusion rather than entertainment, was available, but knowledge obtained from America served chiefly to point out pitfalls to be avoided. Progress began to be substantial after the definite incorporation on 16 December of the British Broadcasting Company and the introduction of Mr J. C. W. Reith as general manager of the undertaking. By the end of January this year 25,000 broadcasting licences had been granted, and the number of experimental licences which, nominally at least, were issued only to genuine amateurs, was rather more.

The First 'Boom'

Improvements both in the quality of the programmes and in the efficiency of transmission were by then becoming known, and with additional stations working at Birmingham and Newcastle the first 'boom' in wireless was observed. By 28 February, the broadcast receiving licences taken out had increased to 53,000, and the demand for sets was rapidly creating a vigorous new industry. In succeeding months more and more people paid BBC royalties and met the requirements of the Post Office by paying for permission to operate their sets, but side by side with this expansion the problem arose of dealing with listeners who, having installed unauthorized equipment or constructed simple but workable sets for themselves, were not in a position to apply for a licence. It was quickly recognized that the complication was too big to be solved by any system of inspection and penalties, and eventually the Postmaster-General appointed a committee to consider broadcasting in all its aspects, and more particularly the contracts and licences which had been or might be granted.

The chief recommendations of the Committee, published about six weeks ago, were that the existing service of the British Broadcasting Company should be continued and extended for two years upon modified terms, that one form of licence at a fee of 10s a year should be issued, and that no protection should be given to the British manufacturers by the licence. Sir Laming Worthington-Evans found it impossible to bring the scheme fully into immediate operation owing to an existing agreement with the British Broadcasting Company, and introduced a compromise, which, though sharply criticized at the time, effectively cleared up the trouble of the 'pirates'. It was provided that persons in possession of unlicensed apparatus should be allowed to purchase special interim licences at a fee of 15s to cover their equipment, and that people who wished to erect their own sets in the future should take out, also at an annual fee of 15s, a constructor's licence. Cynical suggestions that the unlicensed listeners to broadcast entertainments would take no steps to regularize their position proved to be unfounded and at variance with the general honesty of the British public. No fewer than 298,000 new licences were granted in the month of October, and the Broadcasting Company now seems to be assured of a steady and substantial income.

Improvements Expected

There will be much interest in ascertaining the use to which this revenue will be put. The company cannot distribute more than £7,500 a year in dividends on its capital, and any surplus of income over expenditure must be returned to the Postmaster-General. A strong inducement, therefore, is offered for the further development of facilities to bring wireless programmes within the range of crystal detection in parts of the country which at present cannot enjoy the service, and it may be expected that the broadcast programmes will also be enlarged and raised in standard. Striking advances have been made in the first year of broadcasting, but it is agreed that the possibilities of the science has been only superficially explored so far. Experiment, however, has already produced simultaneous broadcasting, and what this can mean is shown by the fact that listeners in Scotland heard the speeches delivered at the Guildhall Banquet last week more distinctly than did the majority of the guests actually present in Guildhall. There is now simultaneous broadcasting of news every night from London through the seven other stations at Birmingham, Manchester, Cardiff, Bournemouth, Newcastle, Glasgow, and Aberdeen, and special symphony concerts from London or Manchester are also regularly brought to the hearing of listeners throughout Great Britain.

In the second year of its history in this country broadcasting should reach the stage when two separate programmes will be sent out on different wave-lengths simultaneously from one station. Experiments are now being conducted to make the project practicable, and when the scheme comes into operation listeners will be able to make their own choice between classical music and dance music (or it may be comic song), between music or a lecture, or between the 'Children's Hour' talk and speeches made in Parliament. This choice of programme would in considerable measure solve the difficulty now presented of pleasing an unseen audience with a wide range in its likes and dislikes.

The aim of the Broadcasting Company from its earliest infancy has been to keep everybody in mind, and, accordingly, in the programmes of a single week there will be found included an all-English symphony concert, ballads, chamber music, dance music, humorous entertainments, news, weather forecasts, children's stories, talks to farmers, followers of football and racing, theatregoers, Boy Scouts and Girl Guides, readings of Shakespeare's plays, a daily 'Women's Hour', religious addresses, and short lectures on a large number of subjects. The extent to which the lectures are appreciated was shown the other day when 5,000 people turned up at Westminster in response to an invitation broadcast by a speaker at the close of his talk to conduct a party through the Houses of Parliament.

The Effect of Echo

Among other experiments which are being made to improve transmission are a series to determine how far echo is detrimental or helpful in broadcasting music and speeches. Two studies are being used for the purpose, one suppressing all echo and the other permitting echo. The present belief is that the elimination of echo is necessary for the best transmission of speech, but that the existence of echo to a limited extent is beneficial in the case of music. Constant investigation is also being made into methods to transmit orchestral music in such a way that every section of the orchestra obtains correct tonal value in reception. Difficulties to be overcome are a tendency towards blurring in loud passages for full orchestra, a similarity of tone between strings and some of the wood wind, and the weird effects produced on the microphone by the percussion instruments.

In the arrangement of future programmes it is probable that more attention will be given to the serious side of broadcasting as distinct from entertainment. Talks in French and other languages will be more numerous, and lessons in languages may be introduced. Specialized forms of news are another possibility. It should not be overlooked, however, that there is education in much of the entertainment provided. Music teachers, it is stated, are warm supporters of broadcasting, as pupils can obtain a knowledge of good music in a pleasant way by listening to wirelessly transmitted performances. There is a general testimony to the formative influence on the minds of young children of the constant hearing of music, good, bad, and indifferent. Young boys and girls with a true ear for music are at an early age discovering that they prefer to hear the 'Siegfried Idyll', the string quartets and trios of Beethoven and Mozart, and fine songs, to the noisy syncopation of jazz tunes.

14 November 1923

UP THE FLEET
AN UNDERGROUND VOYAGE

Ben Jonson once ventured by boat up the Fleet River from Bridewell to Holborn. In his book of *Epigrams* he describes the trip in Elizabethan phrase almost too graphic for modern readers. The twentieth century can still follow his route. Not by boat, it is true, but in a pair of waders, and rainstorms permitting. If you climb down one of the manholes just north of Ludgate Circus you touch the bed of the stream. Wade south a few yards, look up 15 ft or so, and there are the very stone arches of the bridge which until 1764 carried the road from Fleet Street to Ludgate Hill over the Fleet. North and south is the line of the stream up which Ben Jonson pulled his little craft.

After the Great Fire the Fleet was canalized from its mouth up to Holborn. Three bridges, or sets of bridges, crossed it – the Bridewell, the Fleet, and the Oldborne or Holebourne (Holborn). The canal was not much used for shipping, except at its mouth, and its foulness led to the part from Fleet Bridge to Holborn being covered over in 1734–5. About 30 years later the part from Fleet Street to the Thames was likewise covered over.

From our point of vantage under the Fleet Bridge the old bricked-in course to the south is still to be seen in its original state, with the quaint openings up to the gratings in New Bridge Street. Wading down past old Bridewell Bridge to the point where the great flaps prevent the stream from pouring into the Thames is dangerous at any but times of very low level. The southern arch of the Fleet Bridge is obviously much older than the northern. Each is about 24 ft wide, and the span about 12 ft. The paving of Ludgate Circus is only 2 ft above the arches, and it is a tribute to the bridge's strength that it carries modern traffic so well. In order, however, to make quite sure that no omnibus, on descending Ludgate Hill, shall one day find itself in the bed of the Fleet, the London County Council are about to insert another arch close up to the twin arches of the ancient bridge. So, in a few months' time, another bit of old London will have disappeared from sight.

Let the voyager now turn north. He faces what looks like the up-and-down tracks of a tube railway, only the tubes are more egg-shaped. They are the twin culverts put in nearly 200 years ago, and now being entirely renovated, as an unemployment work, with specially made bricks. In renewing the bottom, the bed of the Fleet has had to be excavated to some depth in parts, and some interesting finds have been made. At one place hundreds of broken clay pipes have been turned up. Is this where the barman of some tavern overlooking the Fleet threw out each morning the refuse of the tap-room floor?

At another point scores of skeletons of horses' heads were unearthed. One was so gigantic as to suggest a prehistoric monster, but South Kensington pronounced it to be a mere horse, albeit a giant of its kind. Early records show that in a field near the Fleet the butchers of the City cleaned carcasses and doubtless a knacker's yard was near to this.

Wading up this part of the Fleet is quite easy, so long as the adverse current does not rise above one's knee. How it can fill up in times of storm is shown by the ominous mark high above head level. Here and there, near side entrances into the street, are safety bars placed across for the benefit of any who may be swept down stream by a sudden flood. Accidents happen even now, and used to be more common. *The Times* of 3 October 1839 records one fatality in the Fleet during a storm.

Splashing along in ordinary times, past the sites of the Fleet Prison, one reaches Holborn, where the twin culverts end. Here Sir Christopher Wren built his ornamental bridge over the river in 1674. In the walls is still preserved a series of ancient iron eyes, to which it is generally supposed the barges were tied. From here one can make the underground journey onwards, *via* King's Cross Road and Kentish Town to Flask Walk, Hampstead, almost to Hampstead and Highgate Ponds, the original sources of the river. A short way past Holborn, on the right, a passage leads to where old Hosier Lane used to conduct the traveller to St Bartholomew's Hospital. Sir D'Arcy Power has pictured the sick man coming by barge up the Thames, and along the Fleet, to be landed at Hosier Lane for conveyance to the healing sanctuary.

The course of the Fleet is sweeter now as a decent sewer than ever it was as the 'river of wels' of early times. Literature is full of its odours, and modern London has no cause for complaint that it now lies unsuspected in that strange world underfoot – the London main drainage system.

4 March 1924

THE 'DEATH RAY'

The Air Ministry issued the following statement last night regarding the negotiations which have taken place with Mr

Grindel-Matthews, the inventor of what is termed the 'death-ray', and the action taken to examine the claims put forward by him:

The Air Ministry, as long ago as February last, offered Mr Grindell-Matthews an opportunity to give a demonstration of his apparatus to their representatives and since that date this invitation has been renewed on several occasions. No arrangements for a demonstration were made, however, by Mr Grindell-Matthews until an interview took place between himself and Air Vice-Marshal Sir Geoffrey Salmond at the Air Ministry on Saturday last.

The demonstration actually proposed by the inventor, and shown yesterday, consisted in lighting an 'Osglim' electric lamp, and in stopping at will a small motor-cycle engine from a distance of about 15 yards. The demonstrations were carried out in the inventor's laboratory, all the apparatus being provided and arranged by him. The departmental representatives were shown nothing which would lead them to credit the statements which have appeared in the Press as to the possibilities of the invention, and the conditions under which the demonstrations were made by Mr Matthews were such that it was not possible to form any definite opinion as to the value of the device.

Mr Matthews was accordingly offered an immediate opportunity to demonstrate the stopping, by means of his ray, of a small petrol motor (such as an ordinary motor-cycle engine), to be provided by the Government. He was not asked to disclose any information as to the means by which the rays were produced or the nature of the rays themselves. If this test proved successful, he was to be paid £1,000 immediately, the only condition being that he would allow the Government 14 days to consider the basis of further financial negotiations for the purchase or development of his invention.

Mr Grindell-Matthews has refused this offer, and it is understood that he has left the country.

28 March 1924

'. . . in the inventor's laboratory'
[THE 'DEATH RAY']

[The matter of Grindell-Matthews' 'death ray' was raised in Parliament, where a sceptic pointed out that the Government expert present at this test had stood near the ray and escaped unhurt. The inventor was stung to reply, in a somewhat illogically worded letter, 'Even to the meanest intellect I should have thought it was apparent that the ray unless directly focused on the object of its purpose must be innocuous to those controlling it.' The letter ended on a note which the Government expert must surely have found sinister: 'It was naturally understood that the Government representatives should not be subject to any risk whatever, nor was more than a small fractional part of the power available used. Should, however, they be desirous of testing its death-dealing properties I shall be pleased to oblige them as soon as I am established in my new laboratory, but this, of course, must be at their risk and I will not take any responsibility'.]

PREHISTORIC TOOTH BROKEN

It became known today for the first time that recently in an accident the Hesperopithecus tooth owned by the American Museum of Natural History had been broken in pieces.

The tooth is the only evidence of the man-like ape of prehistoric times which inhabited North America. Fortunately the damage is not irremediable. The tooth has been reconstructed and is still useful for scientific purposes. Before it was broken scientists had made studies of it for many months. It was then decided to make X-ray photographs for examination of the root canals. Several excellent pictures were made, but more were wanted. The accident occurred when the photographer handed the tooth to an assistant, saying, 'Be careful, that is worth a million dollars.' At the word 'million' the assistant's hand trembled and the tooth rolled out of his palm. In snatching at it he struck it against the tiled floor and it was dashed to pieces.

20 February 1925

['Hesperopithecus,' wrote G. Elliot Smith of University College, London, lamenting this loss to science, 'was the first playboy of the Western World'.]

THE 'TELEVISOR'
SUCCESSFUL TEST OF NEW APPARATUS

Members of the Royal Institution and other visitors to a laboratory in an upper room in Frith Street, Soho, on Tuesday saw a demonstration of apparatus invented by Mr J. L. Baird, who claims to have solved the problem of television. They were shown a transmitting machine, consisting of a large wooden revolving disc containing lenses, behind which was a revolving shutter and a light sensitive cell. It was explained that by means of the shutter and lens disc an image of articles or persons standing in front of the machine could be made to pass over the light sensitive cell at a high speed. The current in the cell varies in proportion to the light falling on it, and this varying current is transmitted to a receiver where it controls a light behind an optical arrangement similar to that at the sending end. By this means a point of light is caused to traverse a ground glass screen. The light is dim at the shadows and bright at the high lights, and crosses the screen so rapidly that the whole image appears simultaneously to the eye.

For the purposes of the demonstration the head of a ventriloquist's doll was manipulated as the image to be transmitted, though the human face was also reproduced. First on a receiver in the same room as the transmitter and then on a portable receiver in another room, the visitors were shown recognizable reception of the movements of the dummy head and of a person speaking. The image as transmitted was faint and often blurred, but substantiated a claim that through the 'Televisor', as Mr Baird has named his apparatus, it is possible to transmit and reproduce instantly the details of movement, and such things as the play of expression on the face.

It has yet to be seen to what extent further developments will carry Mr Baird's system towards practical use. He has overcome apparently earlier failures to construct light sensitive cells which would function at the high speed demanded, and as he is now assured of financial support in his work, he will be able to improve and elaborate his apparatus. Application has been made to the Postmaster-General for an experimental broadcasting licence, and trials with the system may shortly be made from a building in St Martin's Lane.

28 January 1926

A FORTUNE FOUNDED ON FANS

A New York telegram announces the death, at the age of 85, of Mr Leopold Schepp, a wealthy American philanthropist and coconut importer. He started business at the age of ten with a capital of 18 cents, buying during the heat of summer a dozen palm-leaf fans at 1½ cents each and retailing them to passengers in tramcars at 3 cents apiece. From these modest beginnings he amassed an enormous fortune.

15 March 1926

A SPORTING DUCHESS

The Duchesse Douairière d'Uzès (who is in her 80th year) this afternoon, before the Rambouillet Civil Court, took the oath as *Lieutenant de Louveterie*.

This is the first time that a woman has held this office, which in early days involved responsibility for the destruction of wolves. Holders are entitled to wear a uniform and must keep a pack of hounds, obtaining in return such privileges as that of hunting wild boars not more than twice a month in the local State forests.

14 July 1926

AN ESCAPED BABOON

An escaped baboon in the booking office of the Crystal Palace High Level (Southern Railway) station yesterday for a time considerably enlivened the proceedings in the morning 'rush' period. After the discreet withdrawal of the booking clerk the monkey, a female, was for several minutes in complete possession of the office, and employed the time first in ransacking it, and then at the window attending to the wants of passengers in her own way. Before she was recaptured many passengers had missed their usual trains, and many others had travelled without tickets, intending to pay at their destinations.

The animal had been consigned in a wooden cage by Messrs De Von and Co., the naturalists, of King's Cross Road, to the private menagerie of Mr H. G. Tyrwhitt Drake at the Crystal Palace. It was described as a dog-faced baboon, about two years old, from Africa. The cage and monkey travelled by train from St Paul's station early yesterday morning, and at the High Level station the cage was put in the combined cloakroom and booking office, 'to be called for'. Soon afterwards, according to the booking clerk, the baboon shook the bars of the cage so violently that it fell over on its side. The monkey then kicked the bottom out of it and sprang up on to the gas bracket, showing her fangs to the clerk, who went away to find help.

Watched by a porter through the ticket window, the baboon was seen to swing off the gas-bracket and make a tour of inspection of the office. She turned out the ticket pigeon-holes and threw the tickets about the floor, opened bags full of copper change money, biting some of the coins to find out if they were good to eat, and, finally, stationed herself at the window and busied herself with the ticket punching machine. The numerous faces now clustered on the safe side of the window perhaps annoyed her, for soon she began to gather tickets and money in handfuls and hurl them out.

The stationmaster appeared, and announced that all who

wished could travel without tickets and pay at the other end. Then he and a porter boarded up the office window, and a little later menagerie-keepers came across from the Crystal Palace, put a sack over the monkey, and took her away.

23 September 1926

THE PERFECT PRISON

VERSAILLES PRISON A certain warder named Masset was on night duty outside the main entrance, and found himself becoming so bored and chilly that he could not resist the temptation to visit a cafe over the way. Being of a gregarious nature, the warder fetched out of a cell – in order to accompany him to the cafe – a man awaiting trial on a charge of murder, and asked a convict serving a sentence of five years for burglary to take his place at the door.

All would have been well had not a policeman passed while Masset and his friend were away, and observed the strange spectacle of a convict smoking a quiet pipe on the pavement outside the prison. He at once arrested the amateur warder, and when Masset returned he found the Commissioner of Police awaiting him. Seeing that all was discovered, Masset at once tendered his resignation, and made a dignified exit before the Commissioner could recover from his indignation and astonishment sufficiently to discharge him.

13 October 1926

A TAX ON GOATS

The previous month Mussolini, in an effort to raise the growth rate of the population and encourage the young to work harder, had announced a tax on bachelors.

After the bachelors, the turn has come now of the goats, on which the Fascist Government yesterday decided to put a new tax.

The thing may at first seem strange. Why a tax on goats? Surely not because the nimble animals are animated, according to La Fontaine, by a 'certain *esprit de liberté*', nor because they deserve the reproach made against the bachelors of being useless to society. Quite the opposite. Goats were rightly defined the 'cows of the poor' because they yield proportionately more and richer milk than cows and cost their owners much less.

The explanation and justification of the tax are given in today's *Corriere della Sera* by a well-known expert in rural and agricultural problems. Goats, he tells us, are very useful if kept in stables or closely watched when in the open; but they may do a lot of harm if left free to browse upon anything they like. It seems, for instance, that they are responsible for the slow process of deforestation on the mountains of the South. Hence the advisability of State intervention in order to control their movements. Goats will no longer be allowed to pasture in certain places if their owners have not previously taken out a special licence and paid a tax of ten lire per head.

Italy, after the Balkan Peninsula, is the country in Europe that has most goats – about 18 to every square mile. It is reckoned that the new tax will be applicable to 2,450,000 head. Its yield, however, will not be so large as that on bachelors. And this, of course, is a just and consoling distinction left to the latter.

7 January 1927

INDIAN BOY FOUND LIVING AMONG WOLVES

ALLAHABAD Herdsmen near Miawana, about 75 miles from here, found a small Indian boy, supposed to be about ten years old, in a wolf's den. From the marks in the den it was obvious that the boy had been living there. He was unable to talk, or to walk properly, but went on all fours, lapped water and ate grass.

The boy has been brought here, put in a special lock-up, and given food and medicine. At night he barked, bit himself and also other people, and had to be tied down. He is very thin and emaciated, but his limbs are otherwise well formed. He has a terrible scar on one side of his face, as if from being mauled by some animal. He is being taken to Bareilly for treatment in a mental hospital.

5 April 1927

[In a subsequent article, commenting that 'Superstition occasionally takes a very cruel form among Indian rustics', it was explained that imbecile children, who were thought to be possessed by demons, were frequently expelled from such communities. A similar case was quoted from *Sport and Adventure in the Indian Jungle* by A. Mervyn Smith, Hurst & Blackett, London, 1904. A few days later, a more detailed description of the Indian wolf child explained that he 'can stand up and walks with some ease, but at times prefers to crawl sitting on his haunches with legs curled up propelling himself forward with the palms of the hands on the ground, and there are also callosities on the hands. His only means of vocal expression, a kind of bark, is continuously and vigorously employed. He is said to betray certain instincts even lower than those of his alleged foster parents.']

'UPSIDE-DOWN' FLIGHT FOR 17 MILES

COLOGNE Herr Fieseler, the German acrobatic flier, flew this afternoon from Cologne to Bonn, a distance of about 17 miles, in an upside-down position. Herr Fieseler recently established a world 'record' for this type of flying

'. . . did not reverse his position'
['UPSIDE-DOWN' FLIGHT FOR 17 MILES]

by maintaining the position for 10 minutes 56 seconds. On this occasion the flight occupied 15 minutes.

Herr Fieseler was accompanied by another aeroplane, the pilot of which testifies to the fact that Herr Fieseler did not reverse his position *en route*. Arriving over Bonn aerodrome, Herr Fieseler gracefully looped into a normal position and made a perfect landing, though it was obvious that he was suffering from the strain of his accomplishment.

22 September 1927

'ORDEAL BY BATTLE' IN A COURT ROOM

Three men were being tried for vagrancy in Yuma (Arizona) police court yesterday when their attorney ventured to assert that Yuma was 'wide open' to gambling and liquor. The chief of police disputed his statement, and demanded a chance to fight him. The Judge thereupon declared the court in recess, and the sheriff was appointed referee. A space was cleared in the court room, and the ordeal by battle began. It ended by the jury declaring the policeman the winner, and acquitting the attorney's clients on the charge of vagrancy.

14 October 1927

LUNACY FOR ALL

The news that the country is going slowly but steadily mad will be received with mixed feelings. The revolution, couched in that statistical form which is now the most powerful of rhetorical devices, has been made in the French Press by a cautiously anonymous but avowedly authoritative statistician. Though his figures do not indicate any immediate crisis in asylum accommodation and do not justify buying straw in the hopes of a rise, they make sufficiently startling reading. In 1859, Lord

Macaulay closed his eyes on a nation which, even if it had often disappointed him by its imperfect acquaintance with elementary facts, had 535 sane citizens to every obvious lunatic. He could sit writing for the praises of posterity, with the year 3000 in his mind, little knowing the trend. In 1897, when Queen Victoria celebrated her Diamond Jubilee, there were but 312 of the sane to cheer her for every one of the insane. There followed the many troubles we all know too well, and by 1926, say the statistics, the sane were but 150 to 1. In 1977, according to these same figures, the proportion will be but 100 to 1, and the reasonable men, upon whose presumed existence so many arguments depend for their very validity, will fight a losing battle throughout the century beginning in the year 2000. 2139 is the ominous year, the year to which future historians will look back as the turning-point, when the numbers of the sane and the mad will be exactly even. The reasonable men will find themselves no longer able to hold their opponents down. The unreasonable will rapidly convert a bare majority into an overwhelming one, and Bedlam will be avenged at last.

It is undeniably an impressive picture, and it is demonstrations such as these which explain the grip that statistics have upon us all. The catastrophe, if it is so regarded, is distant enough to be met philosophically, definite enough to be serious. It is hardly to be expected that eager politicians, and all who are preoccupied in recommending some specific course of action to their fellows, will forgo the chance of explaining any ill-success they meet with as being due to the tendency of the times. All who have a constitutional preference for being on the winning side – and it is the first rule of propaganda that there are many men so made – are no doubt glad to be offered a pleasant choice between declaring themselves members of the party now in power or of the party whose ultimate triumph is statistically assured. The enemies of facile optimism and glib scientific prognostications will find these figures good ammunition for their armoury, but the very people against whom they will use them will also turn the figures to account and call for drastic breaks with a past that has led us to the state of affairs now revealed. There is an argument for everybody in the statistics; and, though they may stand modestly to attention and say they have but done their duty as 100 per cent statistics in being of equal service to all, they and their promulgator may fitly claim a special excellence. They have revealed the existence of a tendency, and there is sure to be a rush of the adventurers who flock to a tendency as to a goldfield. To be noisy advocates of the inevitable has always appealed to a certain temperament hungry for success. The more the figures are studied the more boldly will the slogans call for 'a world safe for insanity', 'looser tiles for all', and 'a bat in every belfry'.

Men of finer mould, whom even victorious bankers cannot command, may yet feel a certain poetic justice in a state of affairs which must be regarded as a triumph for the moon. That satellite in borrowed finery, that Cinderella of the sky, that drawer of water for the earth, will have asserted herself to some purpose by 2139. The sun may still be called the Lord of Life, but the moon will have fittingly secured the last word about the sort of life it is to be, and all who enjoy the fairy tale theme of the triumph of the weaker will feel glad. If certain practical persons of limited range who have been making, for commercial purposes, prolonged studies of the public taste feel the foundations of their world removed beneath them, it cannot be helped. Nothing, they should know, remains the same, as there are abundant classical tags to prove. A people like the British, who have already adventured to the extreme limits set by geography, are likely to welcome the further adventure of national lunacy, to be made in the same gradual but unresisting way. They can always draw back, not by denying the facts but by changing the definitions. But a bold acceptance of their destiny, a genial reluctance to disappoint statisticians who rarely take their disappointments well, will lead rather to an eager impatience for the new epoch to begin – partly in order that comparisons can be made, but chiefly that all may enjoy the 'happiness which madness often hits on and reason and sanity cannot safely be delivered of' to which Polonius alludes in a play which will now be re-read with quickened interest.

14 December 1927

ARTIST'S RETALIATION ON PICTURE FORGER

M. Maurice de Vlaminck, the well-known painter, has taken simple but drastic action against a forger who exhibited canvases signed with his name. M. de Vlaminck went to the gallery in Paris where these pictures were being exhibited, took out a penknife, and cut them to pieces. It is understood that another painter, who had suffered in the same way, is about to bring an action against the exhibitors.

14 February 1928

THE ROCKET CAR WRECKED

BERLIN After attaining a speed of 254 kilometres (158 miles) an hour in a preparatory run yesterday, the attempts of the 'rocket car' on the world's speed record ended in disaster and the presumed death of its occupant – a cat. Owing to uncertainty about the effects of high speed upon the human organism, it had been decided to dispense with a driver, and this principle was adhered to in spite of the reported application for the post by a woman, who gave as her qualification the fact that she had twice been thwarted in attempts at suicide.

The attempt took place on a four-mile track between Burgwedel and Celle, near Hanover. The thousands of spectators were not allowed within 100 yards of the track, but radio listeners throughout Germany heard Herr Fritz von Opel, who spoke into a microphone erected on a bridge across the line. The rockets were ignited by means of a fuse, and the machine dashed off in a cloud of flame and smoke. The trial was timed by means of electric contacts placed at intervals of 250 metres (about 270 yards) along the line, and showed a speed increasing to its maximum after about a mile. Shortly afterwards the automatic brake, worked through a timing device, came into play, and was reinforced by a 'brake-rocket' placed in front of the machine and firing in the opposite direction to the propelling rockets. The speed gradually decreased until, after about two miles, the car stopped and was towed back to the starting point.

Preparations were then made for the attempt on the record. The ten rockets first used were replaced by 30, each said to contain 12.5 kilogrammes (about 27lb) of powder, so that the total amount of explosive substance carried weighed 375 kilogrammes (about 7½cwt). In order to test the effect of the air pressure at high speed upon a living being, a cat was placed in the hood. A mechanic then ignited the fuse and ran for his life. The car disappeared in flame and smoke, more rockets hurtled into the air, and when the smoke had partly cleared, a mass of flaming wreckage, from which loud detonations came, was seen lying to one side of the track, a few yards from the start. There was no sign of the cat. Herren von Opel and Sander, however, are not discouraged by this mishap, and expressed themselves satisfied with the results of the first test.

25 June 1928

BANKER'S FALL FROM WINDOW

Mr Horace F. Poor, president of the Garfield National Bank of New York, fell from a fifth-storey window of a nursing home in New York early yesterday, but his fall was broken, and he escaped with a few bruises.

A woman's cries brought a number of taxi-cab men and

'. . . no sign of the cat'
[THE ROCKET CAR WRECKED]

two policemen running round from Fifth Avenue into 55th Street, to see Mr Poor, who was in pyjamas, dangling head downwards from the window-ledge. Clinging desperately to one of his ankles was Miss Katharine Randolph, a nurse. Her strength was almost gone, but she managed to hold on for a minute or so longer, while the cabmen piled on the pavement cushions from their cabs and a mattress tossed out from a adjacent hotel, and spread a blanket for a landing-net. Then Mr Poor fell. The impact of his weight tore the blanket out of the hands of its holders, but it broke his fall, and the cushions beneath saved him from all but a bruise or two and a few scratches.

Mr Poor had been suffering from a nervous breakdown, and had also undergone a surgical operation.

9 July 1928

[This incident is supposed to be the source of the many stories of stockbrokers throwing themselves from skyscrapers during the great Wall Street crash of 1929. However, see p. 73 below.]

BRIGHTER COWS

The farmers in the State of New York, who are painting their cows in the brightest colours, are not, it seems, to be regarded as ambitious æsthetes. They are normal men with normal vision and are personally satisfied with cows as they are. They recognize that their cattle afford a wide and satisfying range of quiet tones, and that to gild refined cows, to paint the Jersey, is wasteful and ridiculous excess, such as no American farmer would commit just before an election in which his poverty was being loudly proclaimed. The painting is in fact purely defensive. It is to prevent their cows from being mistaken for deer and shot by eager sportsmen. This misunderstanding occurs every year. Often it is rival parties of stalkers that mistake each other for game; but that the farmer can tolerate. What he is determined to stop is the triumphant bagging of his best milkers as they placidly chew the cud. Cows are a mild race, who have long since forgone the dangerous glories of the wild and placed all their pride in dairy produce. They are barterers, only anxious that everybody shall be comfortable, and resolutely comfortable themselves. There is for such an ambling, unheroic community a certain romance in being stalked for hours at a great distance and triumphantly killed with an expensive bullet. That her head will one day be framed as a trophy in some lofty hall is something that can rarely enter the mind of any cow as she sits and ruminates. So the bright colours that are being laid upon their sides in artfully striking patterns, the dazzle painting that is to save their lives, may well seem a somewhat ignoble protection. They may even feel that, when no element of risk to the hunters enters the game, they can offer as good sport as any other animal, so long as they are hunted at a proportionately greater distance.

Last year they were camouflaged upon the opposite principle, in the hope that they would blend imperceptibly with their surroundings; but the keen eyes of the deerstalkers detected movement and their gentle greens and khakis availed the cattle nothing. This year they will look like clowns, but they are more likely to survive. Whether their appearance will have a disconcerting effect upon themselves, whether herds will grow restive and refuse to keep due order in processions from field to field because of each other's patterns, remains to be tested; but it can hardly be expected that the obligation to live at close quarters with bright futurist patterns will not have a marked, and only too possibly a harmful, effect upon that placidity which is one of the cow's most endearing and valuable charms.

10 October 1928

WOMAN'S MASQUERADE AS A MAN

A woman, who had for some years since the War posed as an ex-Army officer, was compelled to disclose her sex a few days ago at Brixton Prison, where she had been taken as a male prisoner, charged with contempt of Court in failing to appear for public examination in bankruptcy. After the disclosure she was removed to the women's prison at Holloway.

The arrest was made on Friday by the tipstaff of the Bankruptcy Court at the Regent Palace Hotel, where the woman, known to the staff as 'Colonel' Barker, had been employed for some months as a restaurant reception clerk. Previously, as 'Captain' Barker, she had conducted a restaurant near Charing Cross Road, and it was as a result of the failure of this venture that bankruptcy proceedings were begun. She had before that been well known as 'Captain' Barker to fellow-members of the National Fascisti, and remained a member until that organization was dispersed. At the headquarters of the National Fascisti 'Captain' Barker, it is stated, often boxed with other members.

Throughout her masquerade she seems to have passed without difficulty as a man. She is described as tall and finely built, though her complexion was considered unusually good for a man, and her voice was not altogether masculine. Neither the solicitor who acted for her in her business affairs nor the tipstaff who arrested her had any suspicion of her sex. Her true identity and the motive for her masquerade have not yet been made known.

6 March 1929

['Colonel' Barker, whose true name was Lillias Irma Valerie Smith, was later sentenced to nine months imprisonment. It transpired that she had married a young woman in a church in Brighton a few years before. The marriage had not been a success.]

'. . . often boxed with other members'
[WOMAN'S MASQUERADE AS A MAN]

'BANK OF ENGLAND', BURNLEY

The title 'Bank of England' in bold stone lettering, which has adorned a small grocery shop in Brown Street, Burnley, for as long as anyone can remember, is now to be removed. Officers of the Bank of England state that their records do not reveal that there was ever a branch of the Bank in Burnley. How the title came to be in its present place, and how it has remained there without interference for a century or more, is a mystery. The property is very old, and has been put to a variety of uses during the last 75 years. It was originally a public house bearing the name 'The Dog and Rat'. The present owner is Mr R. Place, a member of the local town council, and he has been informed by the Bank that the title must be removed without delay. It is understood that the attention of the Bank was brought to the matter by a citizen who took a photograph of the building and sent it to London.

13 August 1929

[The owner of the Bank of England, Mr R. Place, was more fortunately named than the proprietor of a shoe shop in the King's Road, London – a Mr R. Soles.

SMALL EARTHQUAKE IN CHILE

An earthquake shock was felt yesterday between Illapel, to the north, and Talca, to the south, in Chile. No damage was done.

16 August 1929

[Claud Cockburn who, as explained in the Introduction, is believed to have composed the above, left the foreign news room of *The Times* to become New York and Washington correspondent on 31 December 1929.]

BURIED ALIVE

The mystery of the man, the so-called Marquis de Champaubert, who was on Friday found to have been buried alive beside a forest path at Villennes, near Versailles, has been cleared up as to its main features. An ex-convict, named Henri Boulogne, has confessed that he and the dead man were accomplices in this *macabre* affair. From his statement, it is clear that the 'Marquis', who called himself Marcel Clement, and whose real name was Clement Passal, had arranged for himself a mock funeral, which ended in an unexpected and tragic fashion. Boulogne has been detained on a charge of homicide.

Clement Passal, after a life of fraud, was engaged in negotiations for the publication of his memoirs. Apparently the business had not gone very favourably. A man of morbidly romantic imagination, he conceived the idea that the success of his book would be the greater if he could associate himself in the public mind with some striking and extravagant adventure. In conjunction with Henri Boulogne, a former prison companion, he elaborated a scheme for working up a succession of fantastic stories about his detention and torture by a secret society. These entirely fictitious tales he typed out and sent to various newspapers. The plan was to culminate in his being buried alive by the 'secret society' and his discovery, still alive, by journalists and cinema men.

Though the newspapers took no notice of his communications, he carried out his plan to the last detail. He rented a villa near Versailles. Assisted by Boulogne he made himself a coffin which he fitted with a rubber air-pipe. He then prepared letters informing the Press that he had been buried alive and enclosed a plan to indicate the spot. To ensure success the two went through a dress rehearsal to test whether the plan would work, Passal remaining for nine hours in the coffin. Satisfied with the result they then set out in the night for a lonely spot in the woodland road at Versailles which Passal had selected, dug the grave, and put the coffin in it. Passal provisioned it with a few sticks of chocolate and then got into it, dressed only in his shirt, having previously given Boulogne the letters with instructions to post them. Boulogne placed the lid on the coffin and shovelled back the earth, being careful to leave the breathing-tube free. He then went to perform the rest of his task. But being, as he stated, extremely tired, he first went to bed and slept heavily. He awoke late, and made haste to post his letters. Later on, becoming afraid, he went back to see how things were. He called through the tube. To his dismay no answer came, and slowly he realized that Passal must be dead. In fear lest he should be accused of murder, he then took flight.

In the meantime, the letters having reached their destination, the police were informed and the discovery of the body followed. An examination showed that Passal had died of suffocation. The air-tube on which he had relied was quite inadequate for the ventilation of so confined a space, and had merely served to prolong his agonies. Boulogne, who has a long record as a criminal, will be brought before the Examining Magistrate tomorrow, but the police are disposed to credit the general outlines of his story.

The grim irony of Passal's fate is given greater prominence in the Press than has been accorded to any criminal event in recent years, so that the vain desires of the pseudo-Marquis de Champaubert have been fulfilled. Unfortunately for him, even his measure of gratification has come too late.

7 October 1929

WALL STREET RECORD: NEARLY 17,000,000 SHARES SOLD

There has never been such a day of liquidation on the stock markets as this. For the third time in less than a week stocks, good, bad, and indifferent, were thrown upon the market in huge blocks for what they would bring. Prices broke far below the previous low levels of the year, wiping out all the gains of more than 12 months and establishing almost incredibly low new records.

Up to 2 o'clock, in four hours of trading, nearly 14 million shares had been sold, or more than in the whole five hours of last Thursday, when trading was completely demoralized. By the time the market closed at 3 o'clock, the volume was close to 17 million shares, with the recording ticker more than 89 minutes behind the transactions on the floor of the New York Stock Exchange. On the Kerb Market at the close the ticker was 133 minutes behind trading. The total sales there reached a new high total of 7,096,300 shares.

. . . 'A leading industrialist', his identity but thinly disguised under that designation, was interviewed by reporters as he was leaving the Morgan offices. There was no possibility, he said, that the corporations would do what had been feared – namely, withdraw funds from the call money market to meet their month-end requirements. His declaration, however, was unfortunately juxtaposed with an official statement that the Federal Reserve Board was putting credit into the market which would take the place of heavy withdrawals of funds by the corporations. Senator Brookhart, of Iowa, did nothing to calm the excitement by a prediction that, if the stock market decline continued, bank failures throughout the United States might be looked for.

This morning Controller Berry, of New York, announced that the sale of $60,000,000 [£12,000,000] City bonds scheduled for tomorrow had been temporarily postponed because, 'owing to the most demoralized conditions of trading which the Stock Exchange has ever seen, the principal banking houses and financial institutions which had formed syndicates to put in bids have suggested to me that it would be a patriotic move, and in the best interest of the country as a whole, to aid the effort now being made by the large banking institutions' to stabilize the financial situation. After the close of the market it became known that the receivership in the Cuba

'. . . from one of the upper storeys'
[WALL STREET RECORD: NEARLY 17,000,000 SHARES SOLD]

Cane Sugar Company had been made permanent.

One of the incidents of the day was the fatal fall from one of the upper storeys of an apartment house building, in which he lived, of the president of a company whose stock a few months ago sold at 113, and yesterday sold at 4.

30 October 1929

'DINOSAUR' OF TETUAN: A HAY-MAKING MACHINE

The members of the scientific mission from Madrid have completed their examination of the skeleton of the Dinosaur discovered near Tetuan. They have come to the conclusion, pending further investigations, that the remains are not those of a Dinosaur at all. All the evidence points to the mysterious 'reptile' having been a hay-making machine belonging to a Spanish farmer who abandoned his property in 1917 during the Rifi war, and whose scanty agricultural machinery was enveloped in a landslip caused by the heavy rains of that winter.

Although the original investigators were in error in mistaking the curved iron teeth of the automatic rakes for the ribs of a species of Dinosaur known only heretofore in the Rocky Mountains, they were clearly right in giving a Transatlantic origin to their discovery, for the machine bears the name of a well-known Canadian manufacturer of agricultural implements.

Those who, like your Correspondent, are thoroughly conversant with both Dinosaurs and hay-making machines, will realize the great difficulty of distinction, especially when, as in this case, the remains are partly covered with sand.

31 January 1930

[A later article on this episode, deploring the way the

palaeontologists had been duped, declared, 'The only people who will be really pleased will be lovers of classical tags, who can now repeat more smugly than before "Ex Africa Semper Aliquid Novi".']

OLDEST MAN'S ARRIVAL IN AMERICA

Zaro Agha, the aged Kurd, landed in the United States at Providence, Rhode Island, today. His passport, showing the date of his birth as 1774, or two years before the Declaration of Independence, was in order. The public health authorities, having found his general condition good, although showing signs of senility, gave him permission to enter the United States.

The Agha told Press men that he hoped to devote part of the proceeds of his American tour to defraying the expenses of procuring a divorce from his eleventh wife.

19 July 1930

[The following May it was reported that Zaro Agha was taking flying lessons. When asked how he found the experience, he remarked that it was at any rate less dangerous than any of his eleven marriages.]

'GOLD-MAKING' AND REPARATIONS

The Munich 'goldmaking' trial was resumed in Munich today. One of the witnesses, a Hamburg manufacturer, questioned as to the size of a piece of gold produced by Tausend during a demonstration at Gilching, replied, 'I have it here,' and handed a piece of metal the size of a pinhead to the President.

Several other witnesses gave evidence concerning the Gilching demonstration and, although disagreeing as to the size of the product, were unanimous in their opinion of the genuineness of the experiment.

Herr von Lentze, director of the administrative council of the Deutsche Bank and a former Minister of the Prussian Diet, stated that he was sceptical when first told of Tausend's discovery, but that when it was pointed out to him that with the gold thus cheaply manufactured Germany might free herself from the burden of reparation payments he asked himself 'Why not?' He recalled that Frederick the Great had given orders for secret support to be accorded to alchemists in order that the Fatherland might profit by their discoveries.

24 January 1931

[A later, apparently successful trial of Tausend's process was held in the presence of many officials. Everyone present was reported to be delighted, with the exception of the Director of the Mint, who had to sign an official paper certifying the result. 'What do you say,' Tausend asked him, 'now that you see the gold lying there before your eyes?' 'I had rather it was not lying there,' was the reply.

Eventually an investigator found an alloy rich in gold concealed in Tausend's hand, and he was convicted of fraud.]

HITLERIKE

A girl baby of Hilden, in the Rhineland, has just received, from a parent whose political views need no explanation, the first name 'Hitlerike'. The Registrar of Births having refused to enter this name in his records, the father summoned him, and the Court decided that as other defenceless infants had already been named 'Bolshewika' and 'Stahlhelmine', and these names had passed without official demur, 'Hitlerike' must also be admitted to official registration.

7 March 1931

A MYSTERIOUS MR HARRIS

Many people were yesterday made the victims of an elaborate hoax – a day before All Fools' Day. They received a letter, purporting to be written by solicitors, inviting them to be present at a meeting of 'legatees' at Epsom College, to hear the reading of a will made by a former master. The majority of the recipients of the letter seem to have been named Harris, corresponding with that of the mythical testator, but either because the supply of names ran out, or for more subtle reasons, the hoaxers also selected a number of people whose surnames begin with 'D' or 'G'.

Whatever pleasant anticipatory feelings were aroused by the letter were quickly changed to wrath when it was found that the telephone numbers given on the notepaper were those of Mme Tussaud's Exhibition, that the address was that of a boarding house, that no such firm of solicitors existed, and that 'John Sebastian Harris, deceased', had lived and died only in the imagination of the letter-writers.

The letter had properly printed headings. At the top were given the telephone numbers: Welbeck 1832 and 3726; and below were the names: Thomas and Giffard, solicitors, S. H. Thomas, W. L. Giffard, and the address: 13, Nottingham Place, London, W.1. The letter read: 'Dear Sir, – We have to inform you as executors to the estate of John Sebastian Harris, deceased, we are empowered to call a meeting of the legatees under his will, as directed by him in a codicil of that will. As at the time of his decease he was a master at Epsom College, the will will be read there. Can you arrange to be present at this reading and so avoid a number of irksome formalities? It will be held at the Bursary, Epsom College, Epsom, Surrey, at 7.30 p.m. on Tuesday, 31 March 1931. If you are unable to attend, please communicate either with Mr Thomas, who will be at the Bursary all day Tuesday, or with the writer at the above address. – Yours faithfully, for Thomas and Gifford, F. G. Rowse.'

'Gifford' in the signature is spelt differently from the

name given in the heading. The letters appear to have been posted in the North-West district yesterday afternoon.

The secretary to Madame Tussaud's Exhibition stated that between 50 and 60 inquiries had been made by telephone from people named Harris. 'At first,' he said, 'they seemed to think we were the authors of the letter for advertising purposes and were very annoyed, but we assured them that we had had nothing to do with the hoax and had been equally annoyed. We have sent round to the address in Nottingham Place and are assured by the people there that they know nothing of the letter. It is a senseless hoax.'

The bursar of the college, Major W. L. Giffard, said: 'The whole thing is a hoax from beginning to end. There has been no master named John Sebastian Harris at this school, and there is no firm of solicitors named Thomas and Giffard. We have already had six persons call at the college and 20 people have telephoned. Among those who have called is a doctor from Sutton and a lady who has been ill and got up from her bed to come. If the perpetrators are discovered, the question whether there shall be legal action will be considered. I understand the police are making inquiries.'

Between 7 and 7.30 p.m. yesterday a number of people, most of them in motor-cars, arrived at Epsom College. They included professional men (some of whom were doctors), business men, small shopkeepers, and women. The majority of those who called in the afternoon and evening were named Harris, but there were also people whose surnames began with the letters 'C', 'D', and 'G'.

The police are inquiring into the matter, and among those in the Bursar's office at 7.30 p.m., the time mentioned in the letter for 'the reading of the will', was Detective-sergeant Scott.

1 April 1931

[It was reported the following day that an 'old' boy, aged 20, had appeared at the school in a sports car and confessed to the hoax. The Headmaster of Epsom College remarked, 'There are several ways of punishing the offender which would be more effective than any outside action.']

AEROPLANE v. PIGEON

The woman owner of a mansion at Alten, a suburb of Bochum, in the Ruhr, discovered last Wednesday a cardboard box on her doorstep containing a pigeon. In a matchbox attached to the bird's throat was a note demanding £10 by return of pigeon, in default of which the recipient's house would be set on fire.

The Public Prosecutor of Bochum communicated with the Essen-Oberhausen Air Club. On Sunday two aeroplanes appeared over Alten, and the pigeon was released, with a red streamer attached to it for identification purposes. A motor-car full of criminal police was posted on a neighbouring hill. The pigeon made several swift circles over the place of its release before making for home, and the efforts of the two pilots to imitate these are said to have caused the inhabitants of the neighbourhood some concern for their church spire.

Eventually the bird began its journey, was followed and seen to disappear into the dove-cot of a house in Bochum. The observer in one aeroplane photographed it at the moment of entry, while the second observer drew a sketch plan and dropped it to the police. The flying squad drove to the house, entered and found two brothers removing the red streamer. They disclaimed the pigeon's acquaintance, but the incriminating bird, being twice again released from distant points, returned each time to the same house. Eventually the brothers confessed to the authorship of the letter.

21 July 1931

'. . . efforts of the two pilots'
[AEROPLANE v. PIGEON]

WOMAN MOTORIST'S NERVES

BERLIN A special Court which deals with traffic accidents today considered the case of a woman motorist who had made a record bag of pedestrians. Like the famous tailor of the fairy tale, she laid low 'seven at one blow' on the pavement outside Messrs Wertheim's, the big stores in the Leipzigerstrasse.

The defendant's case was that two taxi-cabs coming in the opposite direction, in defiance of a red light, had so frightened her that she knew nothing of what happened. The Court, in a judgment of great fundamental importance, acquitted her, and gave costs against the State, saying that any other driver must have been punished, but that the woman could not be held responsible for her actions because 'she completely lost her head through a sudden shock'. Not having been in such a situation before, it added, she could not know that her nerves would not be equal to it. The Court added the friendly advice to the defendant, in her own interest and that of the public, not to drive a car again.

2 October 1931

HOUSE SET ON FIRE BY WINTER SUN

The joint influences of a warm November sun and a shaving mirror on Saturday caused a fire at Woodley Cottage, Romsey, Hampshire, the home of Colonel E. F. Hall. The sun, shining through the window of the Colonel's dressing room, beat on the shaving mirror – which was of the magnifying variety – which reflected the rays to the curtains. The curtains burst into flames and, falling to the floor, set fire to the skirting and floor boards, which had to be ripped away before the blaze could be extinguished. By experimenting with the mirror the firemen were afterwards able to prove how the fire originated.

23 November 1931

A NURSING HOME AND ITS NEIGHBOURS

A plaintiff in the Paris Courts has been awarded £1,200 damages against a concern situated on the ground floor of the building in which he had a nursing home for the loss of the greater part of his practice owing to the noise from below.

The regulations against noise in France are becoming increasingly severe. But there is reason to believe that on this occasion the Court was somewhat swayed by the fact that the defendants, who are coffin manufacturers, displayed their goods in the window.

5 December 1931

'CRASH-PROOF' AEROPLANE

Several months ago, M. Sauvant, a French airman, announced that he had invented a crash-proof aeroplane, and that in order to show his confidence in the machine he would take it up to several thousand feet and deliberately dive it into the ground. The police have so far foiled every one of his attempts to carry out his promise.

On the first occasion they contented themselves with forbidding the ascent, whereupon M. Sauvant dismantled his machine and secretly, as he thought, took it to another aerodrome. There, a few days later, he was about to take off when the gendarmes appeared and removed a wheel from the undercarriage. He was preparing for the third time to risk his neck at yet another aerodrome when once more the persistent gendarmes appeared with the usual veto.

M. Sauvant is indignant, and has made several bitter remarks about an interpretation of *liberté* which does not allow the demonstration of a perfectly safe invention. If reports are to be trusted, M. Sauvant claims that he has already dropped a model containing a live sheep from a considerable height without killing the sheep. The principle of the invention is based upon the reported discovery by M. Sauvant that if a hen's egg is placed inside an ostrich's egg and dropped from any height, it is only the embryo ostrich that suffers. No explanation of the way in which the smaller egg is inserted in the larger has yet appeared.

17 March 1932

[M. Sauvant eventually achieved his demonstration. See p. 86.]

THE CANDLE-BULLET

The Head Keeper remarked that something was 'as easy as shooting a candle through a barn door'. Most of us who heard him thought it a countryman's trope, indicating the impossible. I have since wondered if it were not a cunning lure. If it was so designed the Gunner was the only one who took it. He declared that he believed that a candle really could be shot through a door and still be a candle when it came out on the other side. He remembered a tale of his grandfather's concerning a man, in the days of black powder and muzzle-loaders, who had won much good October ale by performing the feat to the wonder of the incredulous. Tired as we all were he insisted that the Keeper should be sent for to show how it could be done.

Experiment on the silver-grey oak of the fifteenth-century barn was forbidden by the unscientifically minded proprietor: but the Keeper produced an old spade, the blade of which looked as though it would be just as resisting to penetration by so soft a thing as wax. In the gathering dusk he proceeded methodically with his preparations. He cut off the top of a cartridge and spilled out the shot, leaving the wads in place. Into the top of the case he inserted about 5 in. of candle, just about the diameter of a 12-bore barrel. This he loaded into the gun and took careful aim.

There was a flash and a bang, and we all rushed forward the five yards to the target. There was a hole clean through the spade and round it some traces of wax. The Mathematician retrieved the candle from a bank some 10 yards behind. It was dirty and scratched, but substantially unhurt. Weighed in the gunroom it turned the scales at just over an ounce.

At dinner we discussed the wonder from every point of view. The Mathematician gave the answer. It is all a matter of striking energy and time. When the candle strikes the target something has to give way. There is a race between the striking object and the object struck as to which will give way first. If the target is a brick wall or a piece of armour-plate a couple of inches thick then the candle will break up before sufficient of its energy has been transferred to the target to make a hole. If the target is thin it gives way first, and the candle gets through almost unharmed. A few weeks later he produced his answer in precise terms and a history of the experiment, which has been known for at least 300 years.

In *Some Inquiries into Vulgar and Common Errors*, Sir T. Browne, in 1646, wrote: 'Although it is true that a candle out of a musket will pierce through an inch board . . . yet can few or none believe this much without visible experiment.' In Perry's *Applied Mechanics*, 1898, there is a reference to the fact and an explanation. In an article on 'Collision Dynamics', by Sir George Greenhill, published in *Engineering*, May, 1920, there is a reference to a statement in Moseley's *Illustrations of Mechanics*, 1839, that a tallow candle can be fired through a barn door:

The incredulous experimenter found that a small bit of the candle did certainly find its way through, but he was bespattered by the rebound of the bulk of the tallow. So, too, in model armour-plate experiments, imitated by firing a bullet through wet clay, it is prudent to keep a safe distance.

This statement provoked a letter from Captain T. J. Tresidder, in which he said that in 1907 the experiment had been done for him and that a candle had been repeatedly fired through a ½in. board. In 1922 Major J. H. Hardcastle shot a candle against four deal planks placed 1 ft apart, and then a solid oak beam as a back-stop. The first plank was ⅞ and the following ones ⅝. The candle went through them all and was stopped by the oak beam. The progressive breaking up of the candle was well shown. The first hole was an inch in diameter. The candle had gone through practically undeformed. The hole in the second plank was 2 in. across, for the wax had piled up a bit before it got through. In the third there was a keyhole 5 in. long, while in the fourth the candle had almost entirely broken up, and left its wick behind. When fired against the planks placed touching one another the candle went through the first, but was brought up by the resistance of the solid weight of the wood of the other three.

1 April 1932

INGENIOUS INSURANCE FRAUD

Louis Durand, the author of an ingenious fraud on a life insurance company, was yesterday sentenced to four years' imprisonment at Lyons Assizes. As has already been briefly described, Durand took a well-calculated overdose of quinine and, after successfully simulating death for a day, hid away while the unsuspecting undertaker piously gave the coffin, now loaded with sand, a splendid funeral. The lady who shared Durand's life then collected the insurance money and the couple lived in rustic harmony on a farm which they had bought with the proceeds until M. Durand was recognized and betrayed by a kind friend.

During yesterday's proceedings a neighbour described how, hearing of Durand's death, he had gone to condole with the 'widow'. He found her in the greatest distress sobbing before the body of Durand, who lay motionless with arms crossed on his chest. Noticing that the 'corpse' had beads of sweat upon the brow, the neighbour asked how such things could be, but the widow replied that she had bathed the face with ether, according to the custom of her district. She also added rather sharply that if poor ‘Loulou’ had been alive he would have hated to be touched. The neighbour took the hint and retired. Durand himself, posing as an old friend, accompanied the lady to the insurance office in order to draw the money. It was duly paid in full, although an enterprising member of the company’s staff did his best to persuade the lady to take out a new policy on her own life.

The prisoner admitted yesterday that he had been nearer death from laughter at that moment than at any time during his bout of quinine. His partner to the fraud was sentenced to two years’ imprisonment.

16 June 1932

DEATH OF RIN TIN TIN

Our New York correspondent telegraphs that Rin Tin Tin, the Alsatian dog actor, has died at the age of 14.

Rin Tin Tin is said to have been born during the War in a dug-out in the German front line in France, where he was found with another puppy after a French advance.

For the facts of this part of his life, and of all that followed, his owner, Captain Lee Duncan, is the chief authority. According to him the Alsatian puppy was adopted by him soon after he was found. He was unusually intelligent and unaffected by shell fire. His association with soldiers on active service made him accustomed not only to obeying orders, but to falling into line without orders when familiar movements began.

These characteristics marked Rin Tin Tin out for film work. He was, therefore, trained to make rescues under fire, to save children from drowning, to undertake hazardous tasks, and generally to comport himself as though he were the doggy equivalent of the brave and virtuous hero of early adventure films.

His popularity as a film ‘star’ was almost unique, and at

the height of his popularity he is said to have earned as much as £400 a week for his owner. He is also reported to have been working to the last. He appeared in at least 50 films, including *Rin Tin Tin*, *The Frozen River*, *Rough Waters*, and *Song of Songs*.

12 August 1932

INVENTOR PUSHED OVER A CLIFF

M. Albert Sauvant, the inventor of what he claims is a 'crash-proof' aeroplane, yesterday continued his series of personal demonstrations of the machine by being hurled over an 80ft cliff at Nice. He was badly shaken, and it was at first thought that he had broken an arm, but medical examination showed that he had suffered nothing more serious than severe bruising.

The experiment closely resembled that carried out in March, when M. Sauvant made a vertical drop of 70 ft and emerged unscathed. Yesterday some friends obligingly pushed the machine with him in it over the cliff. After the crash M. Sauvant's friends peered over the ledge, and waited confidently for his triumphant emergence from the wreckage. When it became evident that he was in trouble several men descended by ropes to his rescue. With much difficulty they managed to drag him clear. Later, when he had recovered, M. Sauvant declared that he was delighted with the success of his experiment since he would certainly have been killed in any ordinary machine.

15 August 1932

YO-YO-LATRY

What, then, is the origin of Yo-yo?

Has all this yo-yomania come about because a bell-hop in a Canadian hotel was one day toying idly with an eggcup and a piece of string and discovered casually that it (that is, the egg-cup) could be made to return up the string to the hand? If so, that bell-hop has as much to answer for as the first pair of rabbits introduced into Australia or as the first pair of musquashes introduced into this country. All these pioneers ought to sit down and take thought before they add to the world's pleasures or plagues.

It was a Canadian lady who gave me this account of the origin of yo-yo. We are all inclined to claim for our own country the origin of historical social movements. I am not, however, altogether satisfied that this Canadian claim is good. Another suggestion is that the game comes from the Philippine Islands. The Philippines, it is said, for a long time – for centuries, in fact – kept it to themselves. Then some white man came along and so it got to California. And then the boom. According to this account, the credit, or discredit, goes to the USA and not to Canada. But I prefer not to become enmeshed in these North American rivalries. Anyhow, if the credit for the revival of this kind of top-pastime rebounds to North America, there seems to be some reason for thinking it spread first to Buenos Aires, where the Prince of Wales tried it for the first time.

Well, it has now come to England – and with a vengeance! The country is yo-yo mad. There is no doubt about it. At a big store you may see a cashier in her box indulging in a scarcely surreptitious 'cast'. In another store I saw a fat and ugly woman unashamedly making her yo-yo climb the string like a squirrel. In the commercial travellers' room at yet another great store yo-yo was being resorted to for distraction while the august buyer's attention was awaited. And, now schoolboys and schoolgirls are again out of prison, you can see them everywhere 'walking the dog' along almost the complete length of the string. It has been seen, too, on the lawns of the Squadron Castle at Cowes.

But we must be careful. On a crowded platform at Euston this week I saw the newsboy, in the intervals of newspaper-selling, indulging in a 'cast' or two; and, as grown men indulge just as much almost as juveniles, the vision rose before me of the driver and the stoker of the engine by which I was about to travel also indulging in a 'cast' or two; not only while the engine was at rest, but also while it was in motion. And if newsboys indulge, why should not omnibus conductors? One of the yo-yo player's ambitions, I believe, is to manipulate a yo-yo in both hands simultaneously. Does this leave attention for much else? 'Around the world' is a yo-yo trick performed not without danger to those near at hand.

It really does, therefore, seem that if our public servants like bell-hops, newsboys, omnibus conductors, and engine stokers take violently to yo-yo we shall have to have some restrictions. The yo-yo player, we are told, 'adds to the gaiety and colour of the lives of his friends'. That may be. But we want to retain our lives. Yo-yo by-laws will have to come . . .

The present is apparently the second yo-yo period. The first yo-yo period seems to have extended from about 1790 to 1830. Yo-yo was not then called yo-yo; it was called bandalore. It had other names, one of which was 'quiz', and another (strangely enough) Prince of Wales toy. You can see a specimen in the Cuming Museum, Walworth Road, Southwark. The specimen there shown is said to be of Tunbridge ware and to have been purchased at Peckham Fair in 1821. It is apparently identical with the current yo-yo. And I am told that at a 'Pageant of Fulham in 1834' recently held in Fulham a yo-yo appeared – not an anachronism but a piece of correct period detail. Again, the French make claims. It appears that yo-yo was played under the Terror and was known as 'Emigrette'.

It seems a question whether the bandalore had a concealed spring or not. The Oxford Dictionary defines it as a 'toy containing a coiled spring, which caused it, when thrown down, to rise again to the hand by the winding up of the string by which it was held'. But those who have (or have had) bandalores say that their bandalores have (or had) no spring of any kind, concealed or not concealed.

Some say that each half of the yo-yo is correctly called a

'. . . tried it for the first time.'
[YO-YO-LATRY]

yo, and that the connecting link is rightly called a 'hyphen', but about that I am not quite sure.

12 August 1932

SWINGING THE ARCHES

'Swinging the arches' is an important process in bridge construction. Yesterday the arches were swung at Putney Bridge. It means that the five spans of granite blocks across the river are no longer resting on steel girders, but are supporting themselves. The uninitiated need not be aware of what has happened, for the steel girders are still there. Thousands of people passed by while the arches were being swung and knew nothing about it. 'Swinging the arches' is a misleading title, and anyone but an engineer would probably call it 'tapping the sand boxes'.

The new Putney Bridge is constructed of granite in five arches. During the process of building, the granite blocks are placed in position on steel girders which carry the weight of the arch. At about one-quarter of the distance from the main piers along each arch are five supports on which the girders rest. These supports consist of wooden piles driven deep into the river bed, and on top of each one there is a watertight cylindrical iron box. The box is filled with specially prepared dry sand in which is embedded a plunger on which the girder actually rests. On the lower part of each box are four 'nipples' firmly closed with iron bolts. Yesterday the bolts were removed and the sand taken out of the iron boxes. The girders were thus gradually lowered by one inch and the granite settled in position.

Slow Removal

Gradualness is the most important factor in the work of 'swinging the arches'. The sand was removed from each nipple – of which there are four to each iron box – in small tins about the size of a half-pint measure. In order to obtain an even distribution over the whole length of the bridge during the removal of the sand, one man was employed at each iron box, making 60 men in all for the job. An engine whistle was blown each time sand was to be removed, and this occurred at intervals of about 10 minutes.

The accumulated sand was measured at periods, and throughout the process a large number of engineers was engaged in taking measurements of stresses and strains at various points on the bridge. 'Swinging the arches' is, in fact, a work from which important technical data are obtained.

13 September 1932

TRAGEDY 'KILLED' BY LAUGHTER

A play which seems to be the funniest tragedy ever written was the subject of a lawsuit before a Berlin Court today. Intended to be an earnest and melancholy piece, it was produced in August at a theatre in Unter den Linden, where it was received with hilarious mirth from the audience until, at the tragic *denouement* in the last act, the well-known actor who played the leading part himself broke into loud laughter.

One person did not join in the prevailing mirth – the producer; and he today sued the actor concerned for 1,600 marks damages, alleging that his ill-timed mirth alone had caused the play's first night to be also its last. The defendant urged that the play was not killed by him but was already dead, and produced newspaper criticisms which raised in Court an echo of the first night's merriment. The Bench, accepting his version, dismissed the case and awarded costs against the plaintiff, who, it is understood, does not yet see the joke.

At a performance of the opera *Salome* at Elberfeld on Saturday the audience, by way of contrast, actually dissolved in tears. These were not caused by events on the stage, however, but by tear-gas introduced, it is supposed, by race-conscious Nazis in protest against the appearance of a singer from the Philippines in the name part.

25 October 1932

BURGLAR INTO TAILOR'S DUMMY

From Cologne, a city where truth is often stranger than the films, comes a story of a burglar who vainly sought to escape the consequences of his wrong-doing by means of a subterfuge which has more than once saved Charlie Chaplin and Harold Lloyd from disaster.

The *Kölnische Zeitung* tells how a late passer-by in the neighbourhood of the Hohe Pforte surprised three shop-breakers, who ran away at his approach, leaving a broken shop window. All the wax figures in the window save one had been stripped of clothing, and the intruders on taking flight had left this clothing in a heap on the floor.

The police, summoned by the newcomer, awoke the shop-owner, who was on an upper floor, and he, examining his window, was gratified to find that he had lost nothing. A last look round in the darkness before returning to bed suddenly awakened him to the knowledge that he had even gained something – a clothed dummy which had not previously been there.

This figure, standing in the attitude of studied elegance expected of the waxen inhabitants of shop windows, at first remained obstinately immobile, but when a policeman produced a revolver it came to life and agreed to go quietly.

2 November 1932

THE CHILDREN'S HOUR

It is not surprising that there should have been some acid public comment on the report that the Oxford Union

Society has just carried, by a considerable majority, the motion that 'it will in no circumstances fight for its King and country'. But the critics who take an episode of this kind tragically can have no real understanding of Oxford, or of the very limited part which the Union plays in its life, or (for the matter of that) of the kind of paradoxical theses which it is the age-long habit of youth to propound in its debating societies. Many of us have been guilty in bygone years of maintaining such dubious propositions as, for example, 'that it is better to be a knave than a fool', or 'that this House would prefer a Republic to the Monarchy'. Last week's resolution is perhaps more questionable than these – judged at all events by the canons of taste – at a time when the sacrifices of England, and most notably of Oxford, for King and country are too recent to be easily forgotten. It may tend to perpetuate a completely false imprerssion of the modern undergraduate. To those, then, who are determined to take the result of the debate *au grand sérieux* let it be some consolation that the Union is in no sense representative of the University; that (despite the eminent persons in every generation who have used it as a training-ground for Parliament) it has always been liable to fall into the hands of a little clique of cranks; and that the great body of undergraduates live their life at Oxford without ever concerning themselves about its activities. There is not the very slightest reason to regard its latest resolution as a symptom of universal decadence.

13 February 1933

'UN-GERMAN' BOOKS DESTROYED

About 20,000 'Marxist', pacifist, Jewish, or other 'un-German' books, 'collected' by the Nazi-led students of Berlin University during recent days from public libraries and private owners, were burnt tonight in the Opera Place in Berlin in the presence of Dr Goebbels, the Minister for Propaganda.

The books and periodicals included the works of Pacifists such as Ludwig Renn (particular stress is laid on this type of literature); books with an anti-war message such as Remarque's *All Quiet on the Western Front*; histories of the World War which are Pacifist or defeatist; books criticizing Signor Mussolini or Italian Fascism; all Marxist and Communist publications (including the complete works of Karl Marx and Lenin), books by Jewish authors, such as Leon Feuchtwanger and Emil Ludwig, and works of Thomas Mann (a Nobel Prize-winner), Heinrich Mann, Arnold and Stefan Zweig, and Arthur Schnitzler, and of Anglo-Saxon writers such as Upton Sinclair, Ernest Hemingway, and Jack London. The destruction of books on sex by Dr Magnus Hirschfeld and other books classified as 'obscene' or 'trash' will cause no regret to the great majority of Germans.

The burning began at 11.30. A dozen students, each carrying a book, were shepherded in turn by the Nazi organizers to the microphone, where each recited an appropriate couplet, ending with the words, 'I consign to the flames the writer Emil Ludwig', or whoever the writer was. Then Dr Goebbels stepped into the glare of the searchlights and the bonfire, and declaimed against the 'filth' of the Jewish 'asphalt-literati'.

In place of the literature destroyed a list of desirable books has been compiled and recommended to the public libraries, bookshops, and general public. The list includes books extolling and explaining the principles of National Socialism, books on the theme of 'Nordic Racial Purity', and books romanticizing war and explaining the virtues of a martial training.

The former Crown Prince, who was 51 last Saturday, in collectively thanking his birthday well-wishers through the Press, expresses particular pleasure that they all profess 'joyful and proud confidence in the promising national revival which recent months have brought us'.

11 May 1933

BEES IN HIS BEARD

A unit of the Berlin fire brigade, according to the *8 Uhr-Abendplatt*, was yesterday summoned urgently to the Tiergarten to remove a swarm of bees from the plentiful white beard of an elderly gentleman who had fallen asleep on a shady bench there.

The extinguishing of bees is but one of the tasks which fall to the lot of this indefatigable force. In the winter they have been seen chipping ducks out of the ice, and in the summer are frequently called to remove bees which have swarmed in inconvenient places. Yesterday's alarm, however, is unique in their experience. It appears, according to the account of this trustworthy newspaper, that the elderly gentleman chosen by the bees on this occasion was awakened by their buzzing, but retained sufficient

presence of mind not to make more movement than was necessary, with his lips, to request passers-by to have him released from his plight. They quickly summoned the firemen, the bees were removed and the relieved victim went home.

His name is not given; unwept, unhonoured, but at least unstung, he passes into anonymity as the only man who ever had bees, not in his bonnet, but in his beard.

13 July 1933

THE 'GAYS'

There are two good Suffolk words which I should like to see brought into wider currency. One of them in any case deserves to be set on record because it is not to be found in the NED or in Wright's Dialect Dictionary, in either of which it might reasonably appear. It is 'butterwitch', a local name for 'cockchafer'.

The other word fills a gap in the vocabulary, or might do so with encouragement. I learned it first from my Suffolk landlady who offered me one Sunday the newspaper which she took in on that day. She apologised for its consisting mainly of illustrations, but explained that she bought it because her young people liked to look at the 'gays'. And what were the 'gays'? They are, it appears, the bright creatures of the picture page, mostly female, who live in bathing costumes and pyjamas and lead quite obviously a gay and carefree life, always bathing or about to bathe or having bathed, always laughing and revelling, and always playing up to the camera. Such in general are the 'gays'; and I suggest that there could be no neater name for them. It is native English; it hits them off exactly; and it has about it a touch of good-humoured and tolerant satire which implies that the life led, or supposed to be led, by the 'gays' is not for everybody. A similar genius perhaps gave us 'movies' when those things were first invented.

17 July 1933

DR EINSTEIN ON LOVE AND GRAVITATION

NEW YORK Mr Frank Wall, an earnest student of life in his occupation of reporter on a Long Island City newspaper, recently wrote to Professor Einstein that it seemed to him that, with the earth revolving as it did, 'part of the time a person is standing right side up; part of the time, on the lower side, he is standing upside down, upheld by gravitation; and part of the time he is sticking out on the earth at right-angles, and part of the time at left-angles'.

Would it be reasonable to assume (he asked) that it is while a person is standing on his head – or rather upside down – he falls in love and does other foolish things?

Yesterday he had the following reply in German from Coq-sur-Mer, Belgium:

Very honoured Sir – Falling in love is by no means the most foolish thing mankind does – but gravitation cannot be held responsible for that. – With highest regards, Albert Einstein.

26 July 1933

NAMING A YACHT

Miss May Gould, of Boston, is not the daughter of an Admiralty lawyer and descendant of a long line of Marines for nothing. Nor is she ignorant of what happens to a vessel which goes to sea unchristened. And so yesterday, at Thomaston, Maine, when she failed to break a bottle of champagne over the bows of her father's new schooner yacht as she slid down the ways, Miss Gould ran to the end of the spillway and, accoutred as she was – white linen suit, hat, shoes and all – she plunged into the harbour in pursuit of the vessel. Three hundred feet out she caught up with the yacht, and this time, with a vigorous smash of the bottle that sent champagne streaming all over her bow, christened her *Segochet*.

2 June 1934

THE FATE OF 'DURABLE' MALLOY

Three men were executed last night at Sing Sing prison for the murder of a social derelict named Mike Malloy – 'Durable' Mike Malloy, as he came to be known from his survival of five of their six attempts to murder him. They were an undertaker, the proprietor of a 'speak-easy' in the Bronx, and a fruit-dealer, and they had murdered Malloy in the hope of getting the $1,500 (£300) for which they had insured his life. There was a fourth man in the plot, a chemist temporarily working as a bartender in the 'speak-easy'. He, too, was to have been executed last night, but he was reprieved for a fortnight until his mental condition could be determined.

Malloy was a frequenter of the 'speak-easy', a cadger for drinks. Not suspecting that any attempt would be made to kill him, he fell readily into the plan for insuring his life when he was promised free drinks without limit. The plotters began by plying him with poisoned liquor. All it did was to make him a little drunker than usual. Then they gave him oysters poisoned with wood alcohol, and he seemed to thrive on them. Almost in despair they stupefied him with liquor and drove a taxicab backwards and forwards over his prostrate body. After a few weeks in hospital he was as lively as ever. They then gave him sardine sandwiches filled with chopped tin, and he was grateful.

Turning for a time to another drunkard in whose pockets they put papers identifying him as Malloy they ran a taxicab over him too. But he also survived. They went back to Malloy. They made him drunk again and drugged him. They stripped him bare to the waist, poured water over him and left him out-of-doors all night in winter to get pneumonia. In the morning he had not even so much as a cold. So then they hired a room, and, carrying him there when he was unconscious from drink, they held a tube from a gas jet in his mouth until he was dead beyond question.

9 June 1934

DILLINGER KILLED

The desperado John Dillinger was shot and killed last night by Federal detectives as he came out of a cinema theatre in Chicago. They took no chance of his putting up a fight but shot him from behind point-blank, hitting him once in the head and twice in the body. He died in an ambulance without uttering a word.

Having learned from a woman associate of Dillinger's that he would go to the theatre at 7.30 to see a gangster film, Mr Melvin Purvis, chief of the Chicago detectives of the Department of Justice, waited until Dillinger had entered the place and taken his seat and then stationed 16 of his men outside. Four or five idled about so ostentatiously that the ticket-seller, fearing that they might be gangsters preparing for a raid, summoned the police. The situation was explained to the latter without creating any excitement. They withdrew, but remained in the neighbourhood to see the denouement. Others of the Federal agents were scattered in stores or in parked motor-cars, and a few hid in a dark alley close to the theatre, where a car believed to be Dillinger's had been left.

It was two hours before the ending of the feature picture* signalled the probable emergence of Dillinger. He came, as expected, before the main crowd. If Mr Purvis, who was watching the movement from a car a few feet away, had not spent many hours studying photographs of the outlaw he would never have recognized him, for his face had been altered by plastic surgery and his piercing eyes, his most conspicuous feature, were partly hidden by spectacles, something he had never been known to wear. He had grown a moustache and had dyed that and his hair which had been a tell-tale red, dark brown.

Shot From Behind

As he strolled past Mr Purvis he looked suspiciously at him, but apparently failed to recognize him. He walked a few steps further towards the alley where his car was, then

* *Manhattan Melodrama*, starring William Powell

wheeled sharply. But he was too late. Mr Purvis had already signalled to his men by opening and closing his hand that this was their quarry. A soft-shod detective stole up behind Dillinger from a doorway, set a pistol against his back, and fired. Three other shots were fired by detectives in rapid succession. One of the bullets went wide and gave glancing wounds to two women passers-by.

The other detectives swarmed out of their hiding places. Dillinger staggered a few steps and fell on his face. He fumbled at his belt, trying instinctively rather than consciously to get at the pistol hidden under his waistband. But his strength was gone and it was only a futile gesture. He lived hardly long enough to be put into an ambulance. When his body was examined at the morgue there was some difficulty in making positive identification of him, for he had burned his fingertips with acid to hide their betraying lines, and had plucked out much of the hair from his eyebrows, besides having had the shape of his nose and his cheeks altered.

[A Reuter telegram from Chicago says that after the shooting of Dillinger souvenir hunters dipped handkerchiefs and newspapers in the blood on the pavement.]

24 July 1934

TEN COMMANDMENTS FOR MARRIAGE: A NAZI INJUNCTION

'Ten Commandments for the choice of a Spouse' are issued by the Reich Commission for National Health, in conjunction with the Ministry for the Interior, the Reich Public Health Department, and the racial population department of the National-Socialist Party. They are:

Remember that thou art a German.

Thou shalt not remain single if thou art by inheritance healthy.

Keep thy body pure.

Thou shalt keep spirit and soul pure.

Choose, as a German, only a spouse of the same or of Nordic blood.

In the choice of thy spouse ask about his or her ancestors.

Health is the condition for external beauty.

Marry only for love.

Seek no playmate, but a companion for marriage.

The meaning of marriage lies in a healthy posterity.

Each commandment is accompanied by an explanatory paragraph containing such instructions as 'Never marry the only good member of a bad family.' 'Guard thyself from decay.' 'Keep away from aliens of non-European racial origin.' 'Three or four children are the least needed to secure the existence of the nation.'

25 August 1934

CLOCKWORK MOTORS

The Japanese are reported to be putting on the market a clockwork car. Already one has been invented which will go for 40 miles at one winding, and more is promised. There will be no more trouble about petrol, only the need for strong hands at the key with which to wind up the car once more. On the other hand, the overwound car will be peculiarly useless, and those who have memories of the springs flying out of their clockwork toys will have to overcome an ingrained fear lest the big spring on which they will be sitting should get loose. There will apparently be a lot of winding to be done, because springs soon manage to unwind and announce rather abruptly that they are completely unwound. But motorists will be well advised to welcome the clockwork car not only for cheapness but also for the homely connotations of the name. There is something about the word clockwork which is lacking to words like petrol, gas, or electricity, a note of the nursery which motorists will find extremely useful when they are brought before the Bench. No one is going to believe that a victim could not get out of the way of a clockwork car. It will be contemptible to be run over by it, but no blame will attach to the driver. It will be very interesting to see the reactions of the young to such a car, and to test how far the mania among modern boys for motors is a passion for what is grown-up. It is reasonably certain that the car which goes by elastic will not, if it ever appears on the road, command quite the homage that present-day engines command. It is to be expected and hoped that very different degrees of devotion will be excited by cars according to the nature of their engines. It will then be possible for magistrates to vary their penalties by confining peccant motorists to a particular kind of engine or clockwork or even string.

3 September 1934

WHY RUSSIANS DO NOT SHAVE

The 'shaving situation', says a Reuter message, has become exceedingly sharp in Moscow, where citizens are supposed to go about with their faces hidden behind luxuriant beards. A despairing cry has gone up from suffering multitudes who have been trying to shave with razors of Soviet manufacture.

Pravda writes that there are three reasons why Russians do not shave: (1) laziness; (2) a desire to appear too busy to shave; and (3) fear. Fear, the paper says, is the main reason. Strong men cower before the deadly blunt edges of the Soviet safety razor blade. One man wrote: 'I want to shave, I want to look neat, but the razor blades are too much for me.' He said that the last time he braved one of the blades he stood the torture for a time, but when he was halfway through he could endure it no longer, so he went to work with half his face shaved, although rather hacked up, and the other half growing a beautiful growth of beard.

'. . . the big spring'
[CLOCKWORK MOTORS]

As a result, English razors and blades are highly prized. The gift of a blade marked 'Sheffield' is enough to make a man your friend for life.

19 October 1934

MUFFIN MAN AND HIS BELL

William Fisher, of Westerminster Bridge Road, was summoned under the Metropolitan Police Act, 1839, before Mr Barrington Ward, KC, at the Westminster Police Court yesterday for 'using a noisy instrument' – ringing a handbell – for the purpose of selling muffins at Alderney Street, Pimlico, on Sunday, 7 October.

A police-constable stated that complaints had been made to the police of the annoyance caused by Fisher ringing his handbell. He was cautioned and went away, but 10 minutes later he was ringing again in Cambridge Street, a short distance away.

The Magistrate (to the constable) – You are not going to try and stop the muffin bell, are you? It is one of the most familiar sounds I have heard in London for 45 years. Was the defendant ringing excessively?

The constable – He was ringing it fairly often, sir.

The Magistrate – I thought this was one of the cries of London.

Proceeding to read the section of the Act under which the man was summoned, Mr Barrington-Ward said it ran:

Every person except the guards and postmen belonging to her Majesty's Post Office in the performance of their duty, who shall blow any horn, or use any other noisy instrument for the purpose of calling persons together, or for the purpose of hawking, selling, distributing, or collecting any article whatsoever, or for obtaining money or alms.

'You must have been going up and down some particular street very much,' he said, turning to the defendant. 'Can you not extend the range of your customers?'

The defendant – A lady told me not to knock, but ring gently outside her door.

The Magistrate said that the muffin man was obviously not appreciated in the 'B' Police Division, and advised him to try the 'A' Division. 'What you have to do,' he said, 'is to get wily. Don't ring your bell when there is a policeman about. If you come here again you may be before a magistrate who has not the same views on old street cries as I have. You must not break the law, and the law is that you must not ring. I will let you go with a caution this time.'

2 November 1934

PUPILS AND PIRATES

The following description of the piracy of the steamer Tungchow, *with 70 European school children on board, is written by Mr J. N. Duncan, of the China Inland Mission School, Chefoo, who was in charge of the children.*

HONG-KONG. Providentially children seldom number piracy among their experiences even in Eastern waters. It must be unique to be in charge of a shipload of European boys and girls captured by pirates and delivered unscathed after nearly three days in their hands. Seated now at the very table at which the pirates were sitting only yesterday and writing with a pen which two frenzied pirates had been too blind with excitement to take from my breast pocket, I have written a first-hand account of what took place and of the feelings we experienced throughout the episode.

Seventy children of the China Inland Mission's School at Chefoo embarked at Shanghai under my care and that of four lady teachers on 29 January after their usual winter holiday. That afternoon, nine hours from Shanghai and within sight of one of the best-known lighthouses on the coast, we were pirated while many of the boys and girls were still about upon the deck. At the first sign of a scuffle with the guards, before I realized the full gravity of the situation, I sent them inside, but almost at once I was attacked by a couple of pirates. One brandished a small pistol and the other prodded me vigorously with a wooden holster as if in search of arms. He was too wild to see the notes which I took out for him and soon went on, as his companion had already done. We were all rounded up into the saloon, and before long four frantic pirates were confronting a crowded room full of Europeans who seemed to be as calm as their captors were excited.

Captors and Captured

A few children gave way to alarm, but on the whole we seem to have been possessed by a quiet fearlessness, which was in marked contrast to the imminent danger of stray shots from the brandished weapons of the pirates. During a critical parley of two hours not one of the loaded pistols went off in the crowded room, though only one had its safety catch on. The children remained quiet. Some went off to sleep.

Gradually the pirates' excitement subsided to something nearer the self-possession of their prisoners. The leader of the gang was a hardened young man with seven piracies to his record, who has been a leader for seven out of the 13 years which have passed since, as a lad, he started piracy. He immediately and almost smilingly assented to every request to allow the children to have their supper and go quietly to bed. We saw a little of what was meant by the Master Himself when He said: 'Thou couldest have no power at all against me, except it were given thee from above.'

The four ladies and the 40 children with them in the cabins off the saloon lived in the constant presence of three or four armed pirates, yet for three days they showed great fortitude and kept the children quiet and steady in cramped conditions.

Yesterday afternoon, the third day, we successfully

sneaked across the usual track of coastal vessels and made for a point which the pirates knew. A vain attempt was made to catch two junks in which to set the pirates ashore, and the ship went very close in to land and circled to try to catch the more nimble junks which worked in with wind and current to the shore. At last we captured a junk, into which the pirates began to load their booty.

The Tables Turned

Suddenly an aeroplane appeared, and the men, who had been about to leave in perfect quiet and friendliness, were panic-stricken. The three chief men cut the rope and fled down-wind in the junk, leaving about six of their companions stranded in the ship. We were all unarmed, and the situation was critical, but though the controlling hand of the leader was gone they waited for a boat to be lowered and went off in it.

When they were clear of the ship word was given that we were free, and the girls and boys came out to enjoy a new freedom outside. A second aeroplane arrived, circled round the ship several times, and then flew off to make her report and to send a destroyer to meet us. The last pirates had taken as temporary hostages one officer and the Chinese wireless operator, who had acted most efficiently as interpreter ever since our capture. These and the boat's crew were left on the shore while the pirates fled off inland. When at last the former were back on board full speed was made for Hong-Kong, and we soon met a destroyer which escorted us in.

The manner of the pirates was in some ways paradoxical. They were fierce and pitiless on the one hand, yet kindly and considerate to the children on the other. One of their great pleasures was to call for a basket of oranges and to dole them out to the children. They repeatedly said they did not want passengers' effects, yet they investigated the ladies' cabins and also relieved even the children of all their pocket money except small change. They allowed us regular and perfectly sufficient meals, yet made those of the ladies and girls a most trying ordeal by the proximity of their weapons. The pirates had aimed at seizing $250,000 in notes from the cargo, yet on being disappointed of that they were quite friendly and cheerful and contented themselves with a few hundreds in cash – a mere fraction of what the information of the cargo had cost them.

'An Ill Wind'

A correspondent at Hong-Kong writes:

Perhaps by the time I had boarded the *Tungchow* the strain of the ordeal had, more or less, passed off, but there were certainly no indications of panic or signs of strain among the adults or the school children. I said to one boy of about 10 years of age, 'Have you had any thrills?' He replied 'No, but we've missed a nice lot of lessons!' It's an ill wind that blows no óne any good.

The *Tungchow* finally left to complete her interrupted journey with the children humming 'The Toy Drum Major', 'The Big Bad Wolf', and other tunes played by the Royal Marine Band, which they had been listening to for the previous two hours.

23 February 1935

MOUSE HUNT AND ITS SEQUEL

At about 10 o'clock this morning the inhabitants of the Bacalan quarter of Bordeaux were alarmed by a violent explosion, followed by the appearance of a column of smoke which hung over the town. Beneath it stood the remains of a house, reduced to four tottering walls and a mass of wreckage from which two women and four children, alive but variously damaged, were extricated.

Mme Fauganelle, it appeared, had seen a mouse run across her kitchen floor and vanish into a dark cavity under the sink. But Mme Fauganelle knew a trick worth two of that. Under the excited gaze of her young family she made the poker red-hot and thrust it into the mouse hole, confident that the enemy would be dislodged. Unfortunately, she did not know that her absent husband, a sporting quarryman, had made the space under the sink a magazine for his store of gun cartridges and blasting powder.

5 April 1935

PARADE-GROUND LANGUAGE

An attempt, which sergeant-majors throughout the world will condemn, to curtail the immemorial prerogative of their rank in the matter of hard words, came to a fitting end yesterday with the acquittal of a warrant officer of Austrian dragoons.

One morning in May he missed a pair of new and specially becoming riding breeches and suspected that they had been taken by one of the troopers, as no civilians had been in the barracks. He had the troops paraded and called for the culprit and, as no one stirred in the ranks, he addressed the assembled dragoons in vibrant tones as 'a gang of thieves and a pack of rogues'. Recently some of the dragoons were transferred to an officers' training corps. Being beyond the reach of the sergeant-major they laid a complaint, and yesterday he had to answer charges of exceeding the authority of his rank and casting reflections on the honour of his men. But the Court found that this was far from his intention, and that he had used the words only in a Pickwickian or parade-ground sense in a moment of justifiable indignation.

25 October 1935

PERAMBULATOR MAKER'S STORK

BUDAPEST. A manufacturer of perambulators at Miskolez recently conceived the ingenious plan of engaging a stork as publicity agent. He had a comfortable nest built on the top of an old tree in his courtyard and acquired a stork, which, standing erect in its nest and looming high above the dwarfish houses of the suburban street, became a landmark and attracted the interest of people as they passed.

One day, however, a leading member of the local branch of the Society for the Protection of Animals went to inspect the new resident's quarters, and decided that the stork must have been fastened to the artificial nest. Accordingly he filed a protest with the police, and a dutiful constable was sent to inquire. The manufacturer denied cruelty, and invited the constable to mount a ladder and take a close view of the stork's accommodation. The policemen agreed. When he came within a yard or so of the nest the inhospitable tenant fiercely attacked him and cut him badly in the face, so that he was forced to a hasty retreat.

The unlucky manufacturer has now to face the consequences of his venture in improving on more orthodox methods of publicity. The injured policeman not only associated himself with the allegation of cruelty to a stork but charged the manufacturer with an assault on a public authority which, as he argued, was committed by one of the manufacturer's 'agents' who could not be made personally responsible.

5 December 1935

BOTTLES IN THE SEA

Many years ago now, as I was walking with others along the seashore, our excitement was aroused on espying a small bottle among the seaweed, and on finding in it a paper which bore the message, 'Just sinking; say good-bye to all friends', the name of the ship and the date. At a shipping office in Edinburgh we learned that it was a hoax; there was no ship of such a name, but this was the beginning of my love for sending messages by the sea.

The east coast of Scotland, near North Berwick, where

'I also enclosed a penny stamp'
[BOTTLES IN THE SEA]

the great Bass Rock stands out at the southern entrance to the Firth of Forth, with the May Island not far distant and with Norway as the nearest land to the east, is particularly rocky, so that it is only at high tide and just at the turn of the tide that a message could be successfully sent off in a bottle. I came to the conclusion that a soda-water bottle was the best to be used on account of its strength, size, and shape.

In the bottle I placed a letter addressed to a friend in Cambridgeshire, asking her to let me know at once if she received it. On another piece of paper I wrote a request to anyone who found the bottle to post the letter and to write 'Found on shore' at whatever place the bottle was picked up and the date of posting. I also enclosed a penny stamp, for that was before the 1½d postage came into being. Then, having firmly corked the bottle and put much red sealing-wax on the cork and down the neck of the bottle, to attract attention, as I hoped, I threw the bottle into the sea. The tide had just turned, there was a strong westerly gale, and to my joy I saw my message being safely and rapidly carried out. Five months later I received a letter from Cambridgeshire and also my ocean letter; it had come from Jutland, and the Danish postal authorities had courteously forwarded it free of charge to the addressee. It was thrown into the sea in November and arrived in Jutland in the following April.

Soon afterwards I posted my second letter to a friend in Essex. It took one month to go across Belhaven Bay – four miles from my home – where a fisherman found it and sent it on to Loughton.

Letter No. 3 was posted in the same way and from the same spot. It took nearly seven months to reach Norway, where once again kind people sent it to its destination. I sent it off in December and it was found the next June by a man called Robert Johan Christian Haard at Prest, in Norway.

My next letter, strange to say, once more went north-east and was found by fishermen washing their nets at a place called Sklinden, Risvoer i Namdelen – a small island off the coast of Norway. The fishermen took the letter to an English lady who was working among them. This lady kindly wrote to me and gave me all particulars and the following figures which she got from the lighthouse keeper to show the exact spot where the letter was picked up: long., 65deg. 12min. 5sec. North: lat., 11deg. 0min. 10sec. East. This letter took eight months to reach Norway and arrived at its final destination in Cairo within nine months of having been sent off on 14 July 1907.

After some years I threw letter No. 5 into the sea in the Bay of Biscay on my way home to England from Egypt on board SS *Orontes* off Ushant on 14 April 1910; this one was found at Roscoff, in France, on 28 April, 1910, by a certain Monsieur Derrien, who kindly forwarded it at once to the address in Egypt, which it reached in three weeks.

Once again, in September 1934, I sent off a letter from the coast, near North Berwick, addressed to myself in Yorkshire. After three weeks I received it; the letter had been found at Flamborough Head and was sent on by the finder at once.

Will my last letter, sent off on 15 October 1935, by the River Exe off Exmouth, also reach its destination in Yorkshire? So far all the letters in bottles which I have consigned to the ocean except two have been found and the contents delivered.

3 January 1936

[Not long after this article appeared it was reported that hundreds of bottles had been released into the Oder River from Mahrisch Ostrau in Czechoslovakia, by the German Social Democratic Party. The bottles contained little leaflets on thin paper headed 'For Germany – Against Hitler', appealing to voters not to vote or to make their papers invalid. At the German border the bottles were intercepted by Nazi officials in boats.]

BANK NOTES FORGED IN PRISON

Through the arrest of three former inmates of the San Quentin Prison in California who had been released on parole at various times last year, it became known today that counterfeit $10 bank notes, with which they were plentifully supplied, had actually been manufactured on the prison's own engraving and printing presses. In examining the men's prison records, the Secret Service found that all three had had access to the engraving and printing shops while they were serving their terms.

13 February 1936

'ALSBALD'

A tense situation in the European School of Modern Languages has been sensibly relieved by the announcement that some of its most promising pupils have made a mistake in their German Unseen. It is a comparatively small point – less important for instance than the abandonment of military parades in the Rhineland – but it makes everybody more easy to have a ruling from the German Master. The passage set for translation was to the effect that, when the League of Nations sat down to consider Herr Hitler's breach of the Treaty of Locarno, they must also, and *alsbald*, discuss his proffered alternative. What does *alsbald* mean? The translation generally favoured was 'forthwith', a word always and in any context repugnant to official taste. The Führer however explains that it means 'in due course'. This is a much more comfortable phrase, which is perfectly familiar in Whitehall, and never disturbed the composure of the most fastidious Department of State. The burning question that, it seemed, had to be threshed out simultaneously with a quite different, and equally controversial, issue is seen to be no more than a matter that brooks no delay; and every 'pledged' statesman knows what that means. The embattled diplomatists, who were about to charge *alsbald*-headed into the (of course symbolical) fray, sheathe their fountain pens; and the scholarly stockbroker who thought to win a fortune by hiding the German dictionary is foiled of his *coup*. A crisis is ended, but the vocabulary of nations is enriched. What a word! as the Junior Burgess for Oxford University would say. Why has not English a formula that may mean either 'at once if not sooner', or 'as soon as I feel like it' or even 'wait and see'?

The triumph of *alsbald* is yet one more proof of the advantages of a modern over a classical education. Old-fashioned diplomatists are even now obsessed with the pedantic and joyless narrowness of the dead languages and the old grammars. They mouth over jejune phrases like ὣς τάχιστα and *quam celerrime*, which have but one meaning each; they love the shackles that restrain *jamdudum* to denote 'now and for some time past', and only that. They see in opalescent *alsbald* no more than in monochromatic *ecdum*.

'When I use a word,' Humpty Dumpty said in rather a scornful tone, 'it means just what I choose it to mean – neither more nor less.'

'The question is,' said Alice, 'whether you *can* make words mean so many different things.'

'The question is,' said Humpty Dumpty, 'which is to be Master – that's all.'

Students who have grasped the principle embodied in this main theorem should go on to the corollary that immediately follows it in the textbook. Again Humpty Dumpty is speaking:

I mean by 'impenetrability' that we've had enough of that subject, and it would be just as well if you'd mention what you mean to do next.

And that opens a very large question.

18 March 1936

A SPARROW WHICH SOLD NEWSPAPERS

An unusual murder has happened in Budapest. Its victim was a sparrow, perhaps the most learned and popular sparrow in Budapest and a local celebrity.

'Csuri' (pronounced Chooree) the sparrow was adopted and brought up by a lonely old spinster in charge of a newspaper-stall near the Western Railway Station at Budapest. He was clever, jovial, and business-like, and learned how to accost passers-by and persuade them to take an interest in the world's news. He also took charge of the stalls when his mistress left to deliver the papers to customers in the adjoining houses and shops. He would not be tricked, and rejected buttons scornfully when offered them instead of cash. His fame grew steadily, and as he was cheerful and had the gift of humour he soon attracted admirers and so increased the old woman's business.

Rival newspaper sellers, however, soon began to envy Csuri's salesmanship. As in a liberal State like Hungary they could not apply to a Ministry of Corporations to stop his cut-throat competition, they decided to resort to self-help. One day when Csuri's mistress was on her business round, her small companion was trapped and wilfully murdered by 'persons unknown'.

27 March 1936

DANZIG LEADER AT LEAGUE COUNCIL; A DISCOURTEOUS INCIDENT

When the Council of the League of Nations met yesterday afternoon to deal with the recent incidents at Danzig, the occasion was taken by the German representative of the Free City to make a demonstration in favour of the return of the city to German sovereignty.

Herr Greiser, the President of the Danzig Senate, began in the worst possible taste by expressing his surprise that he should have been summoned to Geneva at such short notice . . .

He said he would speak 'not from the standpoint of the dead letter or of paragraphs, but on behalf of 400,000 Germans, who do not wish to regard themselves as bound eternally to the League of Nations when by blood and race they are bound to Germany'.

Why was their separation from Germany ever effected, he asked. If it was to give Poland access to the sea, he would like to say quite clearly and emphatically that he thought it right and proper that Poland should claim access to the sea. But he was tempted to think that Danzig had been separated from Germany in order to create a permanent centre of trouble and friction between Germany and Poland. He then launched into praise of 'those two great men, Adolf Hitler and Joseph Pilsudski' – leaders of whom he could understand other countries being envious.

Somewhat inconsequently he was complaining a few minutes later that 'democratic law was being violated' in the Free City, and he suggested that a plebiscite should be held on the question whether the population approved the High Commissioner's attitude or not.

Wider Issues

Mr Lester, the League High Commissioner, answered those points made by Herr Greiser which had any connexion with the question on the agenda, but they were not many. It was his duty, he explained, to administer the statute and carry out the 'paragraphs' which were so obnoxious to Herr Greiser.

Mr Eden (in his capacity as President of the Council) expressed his regret at the tone of the speech they had heard from Herr Greiser, and said the correct reply was that they should all express the Council's confidence in the High Commissioner and its entire satisfaction with the way in which he was carrying out his arduous duties. He explained that the Council, and not Mr Lester, had decided to put the Danzig incident on the agenda. As to the regime of the Free City, the Council had not created it.

Herr Greiser's speech had raised wider issues than any of his colleagues would wish to discuss without deep reflection.

After several members had associated themselves with Mr Eden's remarks, Herr Greiser returned to the charge, speaking, as before, in German, and in a voice which filled the hall.

He said that he had now taken 'the first step along the road to revision of the relations between Danzig and the League'. He thanked the *rapporteur* (Mr Eden was *rapporteur* as well as President of the Council) for saying that, though the Council was confining itself that day to the agenda, 'the points which I made in my speech could be considered at a later stage'. 'I regard that,' he added, 'as an expression of the view that the proposals I have made will be considered later.' He said he was speaking 'in the name not only of Danzig, but of the whole German people'.

These words were spoken with great emphasis, as was his concluding sentence that 'the whole German people looks forward to the time when resolutions will be adopted as a result of which the President of the Senate of the Free City will not be called on to appear before the Council of the League of Nations'.

The Nazi Salute

Rising from his seat – speeches are delivered seated at the Council – Herr Greiser walked round the table and shook Mr Eden's hand, after which he gave the Hitler salute. This provoked some laughter, rather derisory and rather loud, in a part of the Press gallery, and the laughter was repeated when Herr Greiser again gave the Hitler salute behind the chair of Colonel Beck, the Polish delegate. Thereupon Herr Greiser, passing on his way out in front of the section of the gallery which had laughed at him, raised his head as if to give the Hitler salute, but instead cocked a snook. An outburst of indignant cries was stilled only when Mr Eden said he had not seen the incident, but that whatever it was he thought it best became their dignity to take no notice.

6 July 1936

[*The Times* was the only newspaper which, in describing Herr Greiser's gesture, specified that he in fact 'cocked a snook'.]

THE SCULPTOR'S CIGARS

Wine undoubtedly improves with age; and when the four figures gracing the memorial 'Austria' fountain in the Freyung Square in Vienna come to be moved in the course of their renovation this week, Austrians will learn, according to the *Oesterreichische-Zeitung am Abend*, whether costly Havana cigars improve or deteriorate with 90 years of storage.

The treasure represents smuggled goods. When the

statues, modelled by Herr Thomas von Schwanthaler and cast in bronze in Munich, were ready for transport to Vienna, the sculptor, an ardent smoker who appreciated Havana cigars (they were imported into Bavaria almost duty-free, whereas the Austrian tobacco monopoly hindered foreign importation almost completely), went to Munich and filled his statues with boxes of cigars before closing them up hermetically with tin sheeting. Unfortunately for him the sculptor caught cold in the post-chaise between Munich and Vienna, and by the time he was well again the figures, firmly mounted and cemented, were surveying the Freyung Square. The Emperor Ferdinand himself honoured the unveiling ceremony in 1846, and Herr Schwanthaler mourned the loss of his cigars – so near yet unattainable – to his dying day.

21 July 1936

TWO CENTENARIANS DIVORCED

Two centenarians of Belgrade, a man of 100 and his wife of 101, recently appeared together in Court to ask, in all amity, for a divorce by mutual consent.

The marriage had lasted 75 years, but only the first 30 of these, the husband asserted, had been really harmonious. Occasional disagreements had marred the next 45. One of his main complaints was that his wife would not accompany him on the long country rambles which were among his chief pleasures; the idea of lonely hiking through coming decades seemed to perturb him. Also, his wife read too many trashy novels. The wife, in her last word, denied these things, admitting only that she had latterly been made a little nervous at the prospect of beginning a new life after she had become so used to the old one.

The Court agreed to the divorce, and the couple left arm in arm.

14 September 1936

US MAGISTRATE'S SUBTLE SENTENCE

American magistrates, in their treatment of minor offenders, often display a sense of humour which makes the reading of police court reports a pleasure. Although pillories no longer stand in the public squares, the old idea that the petty malefactor should be made to look foolish, or that he should be shown the error of his ways in a practical fashion, still persists in this country.

The women of New York are particularly delighted at the punishment recently awarded by Mr Sabbatino, a Brooklyn magistrate, to Samuel Rubenstein, who came before him accused of having maltreated his wife. Mr Rubenstein, who peddles ties in the streets for a living, assumed an attitude of virtuous innocence, and became aggrieved when the magistrate suggested that he might occasionally take his wife out in the evening, retorting that he was tired in the evenings and had no money for dissipation. A remark from the Bench that by spending less on tobacco he might have more to spare for amusement drew the haughty reply that he did not smoke.

Mr Sabbatino, however, was adamant. Observing that a little dissipation might do Mr and Mrs Rubenstein good, he sentenced the prisoner to take his wife to the cinema on 2 December, with the strict condition that he should hold Mrs Rubenstein's hand throughout the performance. If after this treat Mrs Rubenstein still wished to press the case, the magistrate said that he would hear it on 3 December. The women of New York are eager to see whether this subtle sentence will heal the breach between the pedlar and his wife. If it does, Mr Sabbatino may expect to find his time fully occupied with similar cases.

17 November 1936

'TROTTEL' – COSTLY VIENNESE WORD OF ABUSE

Poor citizens of Vienna are reported to have paid 2,000,000 schillings (about £80,000) in lawyers' fees and fines in 1936 for the satisfaction of calling their neighbours 'Trottel!'

The word *Trottel* indicates a condition somewhere between folly and imbecility, but even this does not adequately translate its crushing implications. It has a sting beyond its intrinsic worth. Once 'Trottel' is said honour has no resource other than the law. It can neither be given nor received in a Pickwickian sense. Viennese flesh-and-blood will suffer privation with humour: but 'Trottel' is more than they will stand.

Some 40,000 *Ehrenbeleidigungsverhand-lungen* (honour-defamation suits) occupied the Vienna Courts last year. About 35,000 of them were 'Trottel' cases, the protagonists coming from the poorest classes of the population. The 2,000,000 schillings that this petty litigation cost would have bought 4,000,000 portions of *Gulasch* (the staple meat dish of the Viennese), or have sent 4,000 needy townsmen to the blue Adriatic, or have built 400 new cottages. To pay it the poorest Viennese had to deprive themselves of countless small comforts. The costs in such cases are often borne out of unemployment doles and paid in instalments over several years. This year Court fees were increased, with a deterrent intention, but the number of 'Trottel' cases did not decrease.

Housing conditions in the poorer quarters are often to blame, since where 10 or 15 households share a single wash-house and water-tap tempers fray easily. One thing leads to another, and the other leads to 'Trottel'. Neighbours gather and eventually appear in Court to testify who said it first. These conditions supplied the psychological motive for the great Socialist housing drive in Vienna after the War, a movement abruptly cut short in 1934.

9 January 1937

UNDER THE STARS – THE TALE OF AN INFANT LOST

by **Llewelyn Powys**

The central figure in the following remarkable happening, which occurred in the mountain valley of Switzerland where I am now staying, is today a sturdy peasant boy of 10 years named Andreas.

When he was two and a half years of age he and his brother Hans were taken by their mother one August afternoon to pick whortleberries at the foot of the Aebi wood on the other side of a mountain stream that flows down the Clavadel valley towards Davos. The afternoon was hot, and the mother presently left the baby under the shadow of a rock, telling his little brother, who was five years old, to look after him while she went further into the wood to fill her basket. Hans, who had been minding the cattle all morning, was tired and fell asleep.

When the mother returned the baby had disappeared. Thinking he had strayed off into the underbrush she began making a careful search in the rock's immediate vicinity. Go where they might, however, she and Hans could find no trace of the child. The day drew towards sunset.

Seriously alarmed she sent Hans back to the home chalet to fetch her husband, she herself remaining to call and to seek. Always below her the Sertig's cold torrent tossed its way along its rocky channel, while behind her towered the enormous inaccessible mountain, its dizzy precipitous sides thick grown with the fir trees from which it takes its name. The distraught mother could only explain the mysterious disappearance in one way. Might not the *Steinadler*, the dreaded mountain eagle, have swept down upon her baby and carried it away over glacier and green valley to its eyrie? There was nothing morbid or fantastic about this fear. Peasants in the valley remember occasions when these ferocious birds have swooped suddenly down upon an unwatched baby left to sleep in a swath, and have carried it off before the haymakers were aware of what was taking place.

Slowly the twilight deepened about the mountain. The woman's husband had roused the valley, and before darkness had quite fallen some 30 men had arrived at the place with lanterns. All through the summer night the search was continued. The mother told me that she constantly was hearing the child's voice calling to her, causing her, breathless, to fly through the boscage only to find herself in absolute silence under the uncommunicative trunks of the midnight firs. Sometimes the crying would come to her from the river and sometimes, distinct and actual, from far up the steep sides of the Aebi wood, but always it was calling to her alone and always she alone heard it, audible as the bleating of a kid, if she stood still for a moment to rest her feet, badly blistered from her unaccustomed running.

A little before dawn some policemen arrived with bloodhounds. The trail, picked up at the rock under which the child had been left, led to the trees where the mother must have first disappeared from view, and from there straight up the precipitous mountain side, until the bald heights above the timber-line were reached. Here the baby's little breeches were discovered, and higher still his coat. On and on they went, the mother now tremulous with ever-increasing suspense, until they had reached the very topmost rocks where the marmots sleep out the winter and the chamois with steel-hard hoofs come and go – and it was here at last that the child was found.

Except for his shift he was naked, his legs bruised and bleeding, and he was too weak to utter the faintest sound. As soon, however, as he felt himself once more safe in the strong arms of his mother a radiant expression never left his face. He was very thirsty and when they got down again to the river he wanted to drink; his mother would not allow this, but carried him home, where she made him a warm tea of dried mountain herbs and put him to bed. The child fell into a deep sleep, which lasted for 24 hours. The next afternoon he was following his father in and out of the stables as though nothing unusual had happened.

I have tried by questioning the mother to get some idea

of the little boy's sensations. It must be remembered that he had scarcely ever been out of doors after dark. Always he had been put to sleep in his cradle of carved pine wood surrounded by the darkness of an almost windowless little room traditionally designed to keep out the frost and snow of a long winter. To anyone who has not himself witnessed the blaze of the stars from the mountain tops of the Alps it is impossible to communicate the impression they make of 'a piercing proximity'. Above the timber-line on a clear night a human being has so vivid a sense of sidereal brightness that he seems to belong more nearly to the midnight empyrean than to the obstinate earth upon which he stands. 'The stars glittered. The stars glittered.' *Die Sterne glitzerten. Die Sterne glitzerten* was the only account the little boy ever gave to his mother of his adventure.

8 March 1937

[Llewelyn Powys, writer and freethinker, was the eighth of eleven talented siblings, who included John Cowper the poet and Theodore Francis the novelist. At the time this piece was written he was staying at Davos-Platz in Switzerland, seeking respite from the consumption that had afflicted him since his 25th year. He died two years later.]

MAN PREACHES OWN FUNERAL SERMON

Mr Wade Millman, of Coatesville, Indiana, has achieved his life's ambition. He has preached his own funeral sermon and lives to tell the tale. As he said at the 'funeral service', which was held recently, while 500 people packed the little church and 5,000 more gathered outside: 'This is a very prominent occasion. There never has been no such occasion in the world. Columbus wanted to preach his own sermon. So did Napoleon and Napoleon's wife, but they didn't. I am.'

Mr Millman, who is aged 88, mounted the pulpit to

deliver his own eulogy with a light heart, while the congregation of 'mourners' settled down to be amused. Beneath the pulpit lay the coffin, made from a tree which grew on Mr Millman's farm, around it stood the pallbearers, who had received $5 each for their services. Outside traffic was held up by hundreds of motor-cars parked round the church. Some of those who could not get into the building stood upon the shoulders of others and peered through the windows.

The sermon began with an apology from the preacher for appearing without a collar or tie. As he explained: 'I haven't been able to find a collar or tie since my wife died – in fact I can't find anything any more.' A well-meant suggestion from the congregation that he might marry again was met with the retort: 'Maybe I will.' Getting into his stride, Mr Millman then inquired: 'What is a funeral? Nothing but a description of a man's life. They have no trouble preaching a good man's funeral. It's different with a bad man's funeral. Now I've lived just a moderately moral life. I don't know how to preach a funeral, but I'm doing the best I can.' Later in his address the 'deceased' remarked that he had never worried about anything 'because worrying makes you roll over and wear out the bedclothes'.

After the 'funeral' Mr Millman showed off the splendid new tombstone, which had come all the way from Switzerland for the occasion. 'Ain't that a fine stone?' Mr Millman inquired. 'Didn't I make a fine selection? It's the best in the United States.'

The only shadow on the celebrations was cast by Mr Millman's sister, Mrs Tamar Huber, aged 96, who observed that the 'funeral' was 'the silliest thing she had ever heard of', and refused to attend. Another face was also missing, that of Mr Millman's horse, John, aged 36, who had received an invitation, but was frightened away by the traffic.

2 June 1937

HUMAN EARS FROM CHINA

The Department of Commerce of the United States has faced some difficult decisions in its history, but few have been more tiresome than that of the Chinese ears.

An Indianapolis firm which specializes in the technique of plastic surgery was anxious to import from China three pairs of human ears, in order to experiment with a new process developed by a Chinese surgeon. The laws governing the entry into the United States of persons of Oriental race are extremely strict, and when news of the ears (which will be obtained by some means which have not been disclosed) reached San Francisco, the Collector of Customs there was in a quandary. Was it legal to import three pairs of Chinese ears with no Chinese attached thereto, and if they were allowed to enter what duty should be levied upon them? The Collector, who had no idea of how to classify these original items, turned helplessly to Washington for advice, and after a long interval the reply came back (*via* Indianapolis) that the ears were intended for legitimate scientific research.

Dr Thomas Parran, Chief of the Bureau of Public Health, was then approached, and gave it as his opinion that the importation of the ears would not constitute a threat to the health of the nation. Next the Post Office Department was asked whether the ears might be posted to their destination, but the Department was firm. No ears should pass through the mails; the purchaser must devise his own method of transporting them from San Francisco to Indianapolis. Finally, the Department of Commerce announced that, in spite of their best efforts, they had been unable to find any regulation forbidding the import of ears, and had decided that they should enter the country free of duty. This glad news is now on its way to China.

There is a lurking suspicion, however, that the Department of Commerce and other officials involved may be the victims of a hoax. Doctors say that there are plenty of ears in this country and that in any case there is no difference between American and Chinese ears.

11 June 1937

'PANTIES' FOR BABOONS

Professor Julian Huxley told the guests at a P.E.P. luncheon yesterday that a woman once wrote to the Zoo complaining that the officials were apparently not aware that the sun had made the rocks on Monkey Hill so hot that the baboons had been badly scorched. She offered to knit nether garments for them.

22 October 1937

'POPEYE MEETS ALI BABA'S FORTY THIEVES'

Mr Max Fleischer's character 'Popeye the Sailor' is not, superficially, an attractive one. He has no good looks to recommend him – he is, indeed, somewhat repulsive – he talks in a mumbled, throaty, and egotistical monotone, but he does live up to the maxim that sailors don't care. He is amazingly resourceful, brave with the unthinking nonchalance of those who do not recognise danger when they see it, and he never loses the love and respect of the squawking girl-friend who is the more or less willing companion in his fantastic adventures.

This two-reel colour cartoon shows Mr Fleischer at his most typical. There is no flirtation with poetry, such as there is in Mr Walt Disney's *Lullaby Land*, but there is an ingenuity in invention and a rollicking journey from the start of the film pantomime to the end. Popeye is a coastguard called on to defend a town from a threatened raid by the renowned chief of the robbers. The chief is a great, boisterous, swaggering figure of a man – the perfect foil to Popeye's cockney shrewdness and impudence – but it is less the conflict between the two than the inspired behaviour of what should be inanimate objects as the news of the impending raid is broadcast that holds the attention. The wireless set, after giving its news, shuts itself up, clocks bang the doors on themselves, curtains, chairs, tables, plants perform miracles of self-effacement, and later the magic cave gives Mr Fleischer again the chance to show his remarkable invention. This latest 'Popeye' is good pantomime – and pantomime, after all, is renowned for spectacle, invention, and humour rather than subtlety, satire and wit.

1 January 1938

DOG THAT BIT A BURGLAR

The maxim that every dog is allowed one bite does not apply to burglars in Austria, as a member of that profession has been awarded damages by a Viennese Court for a bite received from a watch-dog while on premises which he was engaged in robbing.

The burglar entered a villa at Perchtoldsdorf, near Vienna, through the kitchen window, made a neat package of jewelry, silver, and other valuables, and prepared to leave, when he was attacked by Rolf, the watch-dog. When the owners of the villa returned they found Rolf standing over the burglar, who had been severely mauled. The police were called, the burglar was bandaged and sewn up, Rolf was rewarded with a large bone, and the burglar with nine months' imprisonment.

On his release he sued the owner of the villa for damages. The law provides that domestic animals known to be vicious must be secured or muzzled. This villa bore a notice, 'Achtung, bissiger Hund!' (warning, dangerous dog). Thus, argued the burglar, it was clear that the owner knew his dog to be dangerous and had still not kept it securely fastened. Whether burglar or postman, tinker or tailor, he claimed, was one in the eyes of the law; a bite was a bite.

The Court could not withstand his logic, the burglar was awarded damages against the man whose property he would have stolen but for the dog, and the villa-owners of Perchtoldsdorf have now all put themselves on the right side of the law by altering their notices from 'Dangerous dog' to 'Dutiful dog'. For there is, in the eyes of the law, all the difference between a bite given in the fulfilment of duty and one administered simply as the result of a nasty disposition, which the law requires to be kept under control.

13 January 1938

SURREALIST ART – STRANGE EXHIBITS IN PARIS

An international exhibition of Surrealist art, organized by MM. André Breton and Paul Eluard, leaders of the movement since its inception in the early twenties, is now open at 140, Rue de Faubourg St Honoré. The visitor will do well to read and ponder M. Breton's definition of Surrealism before viewing its material expression. He says: 'Everything induces the belief that there exists a certain stage of the spirit in which life and death, the real and the imaginary, the past and the future cease to be perceived in contradiction. It would be vain to find any other motive in Surrealism than the hope of determining this stage.'

Precisely what the spectacle, on the opening day, of one of the exhibitors lying on one of the four beds on view had to do with the foregoing definition is not clear to the uninstructed mind. But at least it struck a note of irrelevant fantasy entirely in keeping with most of the exhibits. Here are some of them:

A row of plaster figures representing nude women, to which are attached an astonishing collection of heterogeneous objects such as spoons, fishing nets, broken eggs, and candlesticks.

An open umbrella, beautifully made from sponges. Presumably the bearer is less concerned to shelter himself from the rain than to ensure a steady wetting, neither too great during heavy showers nor too small in the intervals.

An 'aesthetic coat-rack', with the inestimable advantage of being so large that it is visible even when the garments are hung on it.

A large daffodil-like contraption of white linen suspended from the ceiling, the bell-shaped nectary being duplicated by an enormous pair of frilly drawers, which must surely have belonged once to a female circus giant of Victorian days. They are tastefully trimmed with vivid scarlet ribbon some 2in. wide.

A Stool with Stockings

The four beds are notable for little but their mere presence and their equipment with unconscionably dirty and crumpled sheets. No doubt they bear some message for the initiated. Various unrecognizable objects in three dimensions are also on view, together with distorted anatomical objects in profusion. One elegant piece of furniture is a padded stool supported by four silk-stockinged legs with high-heeled shoes on the feet. Even the kitchen is represented by a group of half-opened tins containing plaster imitations of various foodstuffs.

On the two-dimensional plane there are some pictures of ability, many of which convey a nightmare atmosphere with considerable conviction – though here again their inner meaning will be apparent to the elect alone. The work of the Catalan, Salvador Dali, shows a fine appreciation of colour, leaving an impression that he, like a few others, is capable of first-class work in a less esoteric form.

But for the greater part the pictures fail, whether wilfully or not, to reflect the mysticism or imagination which give real value to the works of a Blake. It is difficult, for example, to take seriously a picture whose principal elements are a gigantic soda-water siphon in a rock-studded desert, with a neatly fried egg in one corner and a 10-franc piece supported by a solitary peanut in the other.

A Motor-Car

But there is one triumph. It stands in the courtyard at the entrance to the exhibition, so that visitors are doubly rewarded on their going in and out. It is a real motor-car, bedecked outside with ivy, the headlights full on, glaring with brilliant uselessness into the light of day. In the back seat is a scantily draped female figure with a few pet snails crawling over her. Beside her is a sewing machine, and on the floor a mass of pampas grass and other vegetation, while in front sits the chauffeur, an articulated lay-figure peering through a skeleton shark's jaw set open and visor-like around the face. Best of all, from the inside of the roof falls a continuous torrent of water upon the figures beneath – a more notable invention by which the motorist can carry his own weather with him.

It can hardly be by accident that the catalogue carries with it a photograph of one of the artists in company with Harpo Marx. The motor-car justifies that.

21 January 1938

[The 'motor-car' was in fact Salvador Dali's famous 'Rainy Taxi'.]

HOUSES LIT FREE BY RADIO WAVES

A Hamburg court has just passed judgment on a colony of 400 market gardeners who have been lighting their homes free of cost by tapping the waves emitted by the Hamburg broadcasting station.

The evidence disclosed that an inventive member of the colony was inspired by a magazine article to see what could be done with the electrical energy discharged into the air by the broadcasting station. He succeeded first in lighting a pocket lamp, then a table lamp, and showed all his neighbours how to do likewise. The broadcasting authorities were inclined at first to be amused, but as the number of poachers grew it occurred to them that the strength of the transmission was being lowered by the supply of free light. They accordingly brought the matter before the courts, claiming that the transmission was being weakened by approximately five kilowatts, or 5 per cent of the total energy of the Hamburg broadcasting station. As the production of 100 kilowatts costs the station 250,000m. a year they were being robbed at the rate of 12,500m. annually.

The case gave the Court some trouble. The expert evidence for the prosecution was not very convincing, little experimental work having been done in this field except by the market gardeners. Then, having been satisfied that the current must have come from the field of energy created by the station, the Court found that the law against filching electricity could not be applied because it assumed the use of a cable.

The gardeners were, however, caught out on a law which prescribes the purposes for which the reception of radio broadcasts is permissible and which, unfortunately, omits to mention illumination in the domestic sense.

The three accused, who represented the colony in what was in effect a test case, were fined only 10 marks each, but were warned that such offences became more costly by repetition.

5 February 1938

PRISONERS ESCAPE IN PACKING CASES DISGUISED AS STATUES

LISBON A forger nicknamed 'Balilla' and two companions escaped from the Monsanto Prison here yesterday disguised as statues.

One of the occupations of the Monsanto prisoners is to manufacture toy statuettes. Recently, apparently with the aid of accomplices outside, 'Balilla' secured an order for three large statues. Yesterday, in packing-cases carefully labelled 'Fragile – this side up with care', three statues more lifelike than any by the greatest master sculptors were dispatched from the prison. The empty boxes have been found, but the police are still searching for 'Balilla' and his companions.

31 March 1938

[Lamenting that Balilla and his two friends were 'just too late for acceptance as statues at this year's exhibition at the Royal Academy', a leading article the next day went on: 'Those who remember the beginning of the Boer War may not have forgotten the extraordinary volume of the Boer countries' demand for pianos, which were poured upon them from Europe in unprecedented numbers. The contents of those cases turned out to be instruments of percussion indeed – in fact, rifles and ammunition.']

POULET À LA MODE

After all, the connexion between spring and love would seem to be something more than a mere figment of the imagination of Victorian poets. An Italian, who has reached his fourth decade and all the prudence and wisdom which go hand in hand with the thirties, went into a restaurant and ordered a delicious dinner for himself and six friends. He then lay down on the table, covered his face with mayonnaise sauce, and said to a somewhat startled waiter, 'Carve me just like chicken.' He was rushed to hospital, the saying goes, and explained that he had been crossed in love. The story, no doubt, has a moral for all male lovers and some warnings for all mankind. Perhaps the first and most important, now that the season of cold salmon and cold lobster is fast approaching, is to remember that wise old saying that 'mayonnaise sauce can hide a multitude of things'. Everybody has heard of (and some people are even known to enjoy) a boar's head in aspic; but a mayonnaise of lover's face is a disgusting and faintly terrifying prospect.

8 April 1938

FASCIST FITNESS TESTS

ROME The physical fitness tests for provincial Fascist secretaries and high officials of the Party Directorate, which began yesterday with swimming, were continued this morning with more formidable events under the appraising eye of Signor Mussolini himself. The national leaders were obliged to vault over a 'gym horse', with and without saddle, and over an upright row of bayonets, and were even put through a burning hoop. There were also three optional tests with an armoured car as the obstacle.

Of the 64 competitors only Signor Starace, Secretary of the Fascist Party, with seven others, completed all tests successfully. One competitor was injured after a difficult jump and two others were slightly injured when they failed to clear the bayonets.

2 July 1938

ATLANTIC FLIGHT – ADVENTURE IN £180 MACHINE

Mr Douglas Corrigan, an American, aged 30, landed at Baldonnel Aerodrome, near Dublin, at 2.30 p.m. yesterday, having flown across the Atlantic from New York.

He said he had intended to fly to Los Angeles, and the mistake was due to a miscalculation in setting his compass when leaving. Watchers who saw him leave the Floyd Bennett Field, New York, report, however, that after taking off he set off on an easterly course though he had been expected to turn westward.

After landing at Baldonnel Mr Corrigan said:

'I am pretty tired. I set off with 320 gallons of petrol in the tank, and there are only 40 left. My little aeroplane doesn't cruise at more than 80 to 90 miles an hour.'

The machine in which Mr Corrigan made his flight was a nine-year old monoplane which cost him £180. It is similar to the Spirit of St Louis in which Colonel Lindbergh made his historic crossing. He left Floyd Bennett Field, New York, on Sunday, and the flight took him 28 hours 13 minutes.

The First News

The first definite news of Mr Corrigan after he left New York was when his machine was seen passing over Belfast

'. . . were slightly injured'
[FASCIST FITNESS TESTS]

at 1.8 p.m. yesterday at a height of 3,000 ft. Officials of the Belfast Harbour airport noticed that its registration marks included the letters 'N.Y.' and four figures.

After being welcomed Mr Corrigan left the aerodrome by car for the American Legation in Phoenix Park, Dublin, where he will stay for a few days as the guest of the Minister, Mr John Cudahy.

'Gentle Discipline' to be Administered

Apparently the only person who knew, when Mr Corrigan left the Floyd Bennett Field yesterday morning, that he was gong to try to fly across the Atlantic in emulation of his hero, Colonel Lindbergh, was Mr Corrigan himself. The friend with whom he had stayed since he made his nonchalant non-stop flight across the United States a week ago, Mr Steve Reich, who had barnstormed with him in 1931, was as surprised as everybody else to hear he had flown to Ireland. Every night they had discussed the return flight to the Pacific Coast, and there had been never a word of any other plan.

When he took off at 5.17 a.m. yesterday, Mr Corrigan surprised the few watchers at the aerodrome by continuing in an easterly course after he was expected to turn westward. However, he was soon lost to sight in the haze, and they thought only that he was going to make an exceptionally wide turn. So far as anybody had been able to see he had no food with him, and it was known that he had not eaten anything in all the hours he had waited at the airport. Nor had he apparently received any information about the weather. As for his equipment, he had only a compass, a bank and turn indicator, an oil pressure gauge, and a map of the United States.

Today he is being acclaimed as a hero, another Lindbergh. In the Air Commerce Bureau in Washington it was intimated that the only punishment that would be meted out to him for his foolhardiness would be 'gentle discipline'. The chief of the Bureau (whose name is Mulligan) remarked today: 'It's a great day for the Irish,' and added he had only two worries – how to keep Mr

Corrigan from flying back again, and how to keep other youngsters from trying it.

19 July 1938

[The prodigious feat of 'Wrong-way Corrigan' – as he became known, echoing the nickname of Californian footballer 'Wrong-way' Riegles, who had scored a famous own goal nine years earlier – is all the more remarkable for its taking place only eleven years after the first-ever aerial crossing of the Atlantic by Charles Lindbergh. Meanwhile, elaborate plans were being laid for a commercial transatlantic air service involving an unlikely looking combination of two seaplanes riding piggy-back one above the other, named the Short 'Mayo'. The powerful 'mother' seaplane would, it was hoped, lift the passenger-carrying machine to a respectable height, so that the latter, when released, could continue on its way in level flight until its transatlantic fuel load had lightened sufficiently to enable it to climb. Corrigan made all these preparations look rather silly.]

MAN POSTS HIMSELF AS A PARCEL

THE HAGUE Packed neatly in a large and correctly labelled case, an Englishman whose name is given as Mr W. M. Edwards has just arrived safely in Amsterdam from London by air parcel post on board a machine of the International Air Freight Limited.

Asked to account for his behaviour, Mr Edwards explained that, having missed the regular passenger plane, he hit upon this novel method of arriving in Amsterdam in time to keep a pressing appointment.

25 August 1938

'HAPPIEST NEWS FOR 20 YEARS'

COPENHAGEN The *Politiken's* headline this morning expresses the Danish people's joy in what it calls 'the happiest piece of news in 20 eventful years'. In its leading article it praises 'Old Man Chamberlain, who would not give up and created a new kind of international conference by telegraphing to Herr Hitler: "May I come and see you?" ' The *Berlingske Tidende*, however, gives expression to some anxiety when it states:

> There will be some, specially among the small nations, who in the midst of their joy that the avalanche has been stopped and heaven's light preserved will feel a cold shiver.

1 October 1938

THE BALLOON AND THE CHILDREN

From the window it looked as though the moon had been caught in the rusty foliage of Battersea Park; something large and round and silver could be seen struggling faintly among the tree-tops. Closer inspection revealed the balloon, still flaccid and half-inflated, but dwarfing with its heavy bulk the two lorries, one loaded with scarlet gas cylinders, its posse of cheerful attendants who were hauling on a complicated system of guide-ropes and crawling about underneath the belly of the monster, and the large crowd of spectators which stood round open-mouthed in the pale autumn sunshine.

The crowd in this park was mostly children. Boys clambered on the railings and rode precarious bicycles through the fringes of the throng showing off in front of the sisters of their friends, who stood, generally with a perambulator, and stared steadily on the spectacle, ignoring the other sex. The inmates of the perambulators almost with one accord took a pessimistic view of the whole business. They howled continuously and were deaf to the appeals of their sisters to 'look at the pretty balloon', which they obviously regarded as a portent of the worst possible kind.

It seemed long before anything happened, but the crowd did not disperse. One group of small boys was suddenly enlivened by the advent of its natural leader. 'Ere's Smooger!' 'Good old Smooger!' they yelled. ' 'Ave yer seen the balloon?' Smooger was not impressed. 'I seen plenty,' he remarked. 'There's one gone up just down our street.' It gradually dawned on us that ours was not the only balloon in London; from where we stood we could count five already in the sky. Smooger became technical. 'See that on the lorry? That's the winch. Run off an engine that is.' But his lecture was interrupted. There was a loud and prolonged hiss from the scene of operations, and a universal cry of 'Coo, 'ark at the gas!' The balloon swelled visibly, its creases filled out, and it became immense, plethoric, and much more difficult to manage. Some of the crew hung firmly on to the guide-ropes, while others ran about making last-minute adjustments. One man climbed up on to the lorry and tested the running of the winch. The gas-cylinders were disconnected, and as the crew slowly released the guide-ropes through pulleys, the balloon began to rise off the ground. Until now its rotundity had been marred by the loose untidy folds which draped one end, and looked rather like the exaggeratedly flowing tail-fins of an exotic goldfish. But as the wind filled them, these fins suddenly grew elephantine and muscular, and we realized that they were 'meant to be like that', and that there was no gas shortage.

By now the balloon had risen 30 ft or 40 ft above the crowd, and was dancing a large and unwieldy *pas seul* above the tree-tops, the guide-ropes swinging together from its waist like a very exiguous skirt. The end of the long trailing gas tube was secured in a neat little canvas bag, and a gay scarlet and white wind-sock was fastened to the cable. Then, at a last order, the winch began to run steadily, and our balloon climbed majestically up a steep slant away from the upturned faces of the crowd towards its brethren in the skies.

10 October 1938

PANIC CAUSED BY BROADCAST

America today hardly knows whether to laugh or to be angry. Here is a nation which, alone of big nations, has deemed it unnecessary to rehearse for protection against attack from the air by fellow-beings on this earth and suddenly believes itself – and for little enough reason – faced with a more fearful attack from another world.

All began after 8 o'clock last night, when a dramatization of Mr H. G. Wells's fantasy *The War of the Worlds* came on the air over the national 'network' of the Columbia broadcasting system. The programme was the work of Mr Orson Welles, a young American who is known as an innovator on the New York stage. He dramatizes a book or a play every Sunday night on the wireless.

The story, written before bombers became a reality on this world, was presented with an American locale substituted for the English. The programme opened with the usual announcements, and Mr Orson Welles described the series of which it is a part. Then a setting was built up, first a weather report, then a programme of dance music from a fictitious hotel. In the middle of a number came a 'flash' about an astronomer having observed a gas explosion on Mars. News bulletins and descriptive broadcasts followed rapidly – just as in the recent European crisis. A 'meteor' had landed near Princeton, New Jersey, killing 1,500 persons. No, it was not a meteor, it was a 'metal cylinder' – and the top unscrewed – and monsters crawled out armed with death rays – and they were impervious to bullets – and they were marching on New York – and martial law had been declared and State militia were out. And so on, all told in a voice of doom.

'. . . hurried into the streets'
[PANIC CAUSED BY BROADCAST]

Towels As Gas Masks

Thrice after the initial announcement it was explained that the events were only part of a wireless programme, but these were insufficient to arrest panic in many peaceful Sunday night homes. Telephone lines to police stations, newspaper offices, and broadcasting stations were soon jammed; in some towns people hurried into the streets, many with towels over their faces as gas masks. Less excitable citizens telephoned to the authorities to know how they could help in the emergency. Even church services were interrupted.

This state of affairs continued until a series of reassuring announcements by the Columbia officials and the police and news services restored peace.

The upshot today is that the Federal Communications Commission, which issues all licences for broadcasting, has asked for the script of the broadcast and for the electrical recording taken at the time. The chairman has declared that any programme causing such panic is at least regrettable, and that he will institute a prompt inquiry.

Mr. H. G. Wells's literary representative in New York stated today that he gave permission for one performance of *The War of the Worlds* over the wireless, but it was not explained to him that there would be rewriting which would turn it 'into an entirely different story'. He added that Mr Wells and himself were deeply concerned, and considered retraction was necessary by the Columbia Company and Mr Orson Welles.

1 November 1938

MRS MINIVER IN NOVEMBER – A WILD DAY

Looking up casually in the middle of writing a letter, Mrs Miniver saw, through the back window of the drawing-room, something that she had never consciously seen before: the last leaf being blown from a tree. One moment it was there, on the highest bough of all, wagging wildly in the wind and the rain. The next moment it was whirling away across the roof tops, a forlorn ragged speck. The line of its flight was the arabesque at the end of a chapter, the final scroll under the death-warrant of summer. Once more the lime tree stood bone-naked.

So that was that, thought Mrs Miniver; and a good thing, too. At first, like most people, she had enjoyed the amazing spell of warm weather which had lasted throughout October and most of November. It had been pleasant and comforting; it had helped to heal the scars which the last fortnight of September had left behind. But later, as day after day broke close and windless, and night after night failed to bring any refreshing chill, Mrs Miniver began to feel oddly uneasy. The year, now, seemed like an ageing woman whose smooth cheeks were the result, not of a heart perennially young, but of an assured income, a sound digestion, and a protective callousness of spirit. Out of those too-bright eyes there looked, now, not youthfulness, but infantilism; and the smile which accompanied the look was growing a little vacant.

It had been a great relief, therefore, when, a few days before, the weather had broken with a spectacular gale. The old beautiful painted aristocracy of the leaves, already tottering, had fallen in a night, overthrown by outward pressure and inward decadence. What remained were the essential masses of the tree, bare and sober, with a workaday beauty of their own. Through them, after a while, the sap would rise into a new aristocracy, which would flourish until it, too, had lost its freshness; and then fall. There was no other way, it seemed, in a deciduous world. True evergreenness did not exist: the word was only another term for the ability to overlap the old with the new.

By the time she had finished her letter, which was a long one to Vin, the rain had nearly stopped, though the gale was as strong as ever. She put on a mackintosh and struggled up the square to the pillar-box. Outside the little newsagent's the evening paper placards were flapping under their wire grids like netted geese. The lower half of one of them had been folded upwards by the wind, hiding everything except the word 'JEWS'. Mrs Miniver was conscious of an instantaneous mental wincing, and an almost intantaneous remorse for it. However long the horror continued, one must not get to the stage of refusing to think about it. To shrink from direct pain was bad enough, but to shrink from vicarious pain was the ultimate cowardice. And whereas to conceal direct pain was a virtue, to conceal vicarious pain was a sin. Only by feeling it to the utmost, and by expressing it, could the rest of the world help to heal the injury which had caused it. Money, food, clothing, shelter – people could give all these and still it would not be enough: it would not absolve them from the duty of paying in full, also, the imponderable tribute of grief.

She turned down the next street towards the river. It was Nannie's day out and she was going to fetch the children from school. The Royal Hospital, with bare straining trees in front of it and black flying clouds behind, stood sombrely magnificent, a fitting backcloth for the latest tragedy of the world. And here, perhaps, thought Mrs Miniver, battling along St Leonard's Terrace under the lee of the wall, was a clue to the uneasiness which she had felt at the lingering on of summer. All the associations of November, the traditional flotsam left upon its shore by the successive tides of history, went ill with halcyon weather. It was the wind-month, the blood-month, Brumaire, the month of darkness: its sign was the evil scorpion, who, when surrounded by a ring of fire, was said to sting itself and die of its own poison. It was ushered in by the Vigil of Saman, Lord of Death, by the witches and warlocks of Hallowe'en. A later tide had left a later mark – the ritual bonfires of Guy Fawkes' Day, round which children still stood in primitive excitement, their innocent eyes reflecting unconsciously the twin flames of sadism and fire-worship. This year, down at Starlings, the farmer's children next door had made an extra large bonfire, and for the Guy's face they had used a mask representing the wicked Queen out of Disney's 'Seven Dwarfs', which Joey

Iggulsden had bought at the village shop. This blend of two nursery ideologies, 300 years apart, had particularly appealed to Clem. It showed, he said, that children had an inborn knowledge that evil was evil, irrespective of time or place; but Vin said it only showed that Joey Iggulsden had a sense of humour. Anyway, it had been a grand bonfire, of a terrifying heat and redness. Watching it, Mrs Miniver had tried for a few moments to treat the scene as a reality, and found herself wondering whether there was any cause or conviction in the world for which she would have the courage to go to the stake. She could think of several for which she would make the attempt; but, as the effigy lurched forward suddenly from the waist, with forked flames issuing from its sleeves like burning fingers, and its painted leer crumpling and writhing in the heat, she shuddered, and admitted, humbly enough, that she herself would probably recant at the crackling of the first twig.

However, nobody nowadays was burnt at the stake. The unfortunate ones of the world were subjected to a more lingering torment, and the fortunate ones were merely condemned to watch it from a front seat, unwilling *tricoteuses* at an execution they were powerless to prevent. The least they could do was not to turn away their eyes; for with such a picture stamped upon the retina of their memory they would not be able to lie easy, the fortunate ones, until they had done their best to ensure that it could never happen again. But it was going to leave yet another ineffaceable watermark on the bleak shores of November.

When she reached the Embankment she met the full force of the gale, and exulted in it. Yes, this was the kind of weather that the events of the world called for: a wild, dark day, suitable for a wild, dark mood. From the two tall chimneys of the power station the smoke streamed out horizontally, a black banner and a white one. The river was at the three-quarter flood. It looked like a battlefield, water and wind meeting angrily in a thousand small hand-to-hand contests. But in an hour or so the tide would turn.

29 November 1938

[Mrs Miniver, with her curious blend of gentility and pluck, first appeared in *The Times*, and soon became something of a national heroine: a symbol of British womanhood's defiance of the Nazi threat. The book *Mrs Miniver* by Jan Struther was published in 1939, and in 1942 William Wyler directed the film *Mrs Miniver* for MGM. The film critic Eric Rhode remarked of a scene in this film: 'Mrs Miniver may project responsibility for destruction on to the enemy, as most war propaganda does, but this scene intimates that war symbolizes the destructive impulse in everyone, and that nearly everyone at one time or another wishes to blitz a home of Mrs Miniver's kind.']

ROAST VEAL 100 YEARS OLD

In the museum of the Royal United Service Institution in Whitehall may now be seen a glass tube containing roast veal taken from a tin more than 100 years old. The tin is also on exhibition, with the formidable instruction: 'Cut round with chisel and hammer'.

The tin is the earliest known example of canned food, and is one of the exhibits at the museum connected with polar exploration. It formed part of the stores taken by Sir William Parry on his expedition to the Arctic in 1824 and brought back unused.

Last year, at the request of the International Tin Research and Development Council, the museum authorities sanctioned the opening of the tin so that a chemical and bacteriological examination might be made of the contents. No trace of preservatives was detected. The contents of the tin were found in perfect condition: some of the meat was given to a cat without ill effects, and 10 rats which were fed on it for some days provided a testimonial to its quality by putting on weight during the period.

Although a Frenchman invented the process of canning

at the end of the eighteenth century, it was left to the English firm of Donkin and Hall to make practical use of his discovery. The firm set up business in 1811, and two years later their products were being used by the Navy and Army. It is reported that the Duke of Wellington, then Lord Wellesley, tried and approved of their preserved beef, and in 1814 Sir Joseph Banks, then president of the Royal Society, wrote in praise of the nutritious qualities of what he termed 'your embalmed provisions'.

It was in this year also that the firm supplied the expedition to Baffin's Bay which Parry accompanied as a lieutenant, and five years later, on his first voyage to discover the north-west passage, canned meat, soup, and vegetables formed a valuable aid in combating scurvy.

4 February 1939

WINDING UP THE CLOCK

In a recent police-court case a man stated that his mother-in-law had several times taken down the clock from the sideboard, wound it up, and then thrown it at him. This item of news has a double interest. First, it shows that the good old race of mothers-in-law is still breeding true to type: which, in a world of change and bewilderment, is a reassuring sign. Secondly, it brings to our notice an important refinement in the technique of domestic brawls. '*Wound it up*': those are the significant words. For the insultingness of missiles (as distinct from their injuriousness) is directly proportionate to the value which the thrower sets upon them. To heave a book, though less dangerous, is far more offensive than to heave a brick; and, of two books, a small volume of Shakespeare's Sonnets in white vellum is much more morally wounding than a telephone directory. An earthenware pudding-basin may crack the skull; but a delicate porcelain tea-cup, if willingly sacrificed in the cause of enmity, will inflict a deeper gash upon the sensitive soul.

It is the same with clocks. As everybody knows, a clock is one of the most satisfactory missiles in the world. It is hard, heavy, and angular, and when it falls there is a splendid crash of glass and a sinister twangling sound as its steely entrails spill themselves out upon the floor. Even a clock which no longer goes, and which is only kept on the mantelpiece (or the sideboard) for ornamental or sentimental reasons, is a pretty good thing to throw: but a practicable clock, a clock in perfect working order, a clock on which everybody in the house depends – that is the best projectile of all. And that, no doubt, is why this particular mother-in-law, with calculated devilry, wound it up first. She wanted her son-in-law to see for himself how valuable an object she was about to destroy, how much expense and inconvenience she was willing to incur, for the pleasure of dotting him one. The measure of her sacrifice was to be the measure of her contempt.

All honour to her. In her own line she is a very considerable artist.

25 February 1939

THE MODEL NAZI HUMORIST

BERLIN The first prize of 100 marks in the competition organized by the *Angriff*, the most radical of the Nazi Party newspapers, with the object of proving that Germans possess a sense of humour has been won, it was announced this evening, by Herr Kurt Naumann, a builder's labourer, who contributes three jokes illustrated by his own drawings.

The first of these drawings represents a very scantily clad dancer confronted by an astonished theatre director and bears the caption, 'I won't go on in this costume.' 'Why, does it show too much?' 'No, you old fool, too little.' The second drawing which appealed to the judges is one of a woman in an extremely short dress, who is shown saying to her husband: 'You haven't looked at my new dress. I am buying it by instalments,' to which the man answers: 'I suppose that is the first instalment that you are wearing.' The third winning joke shows a bloated pug saying to a meagre dachshund: 'How thin you have got, Fifi!' and receiving the answer: 'I was sold to a vegetarian three weeks ago.'

The second and fourth prizes in the competition, amounting to 75m. and 25m. respectively, were won by women, the third prize of 50m. by a man. Their jokes have not yet been published, but readers are promised an assortment for tomorrow.

In their remarks on the awards the judges make it clear that, in spite of the title of the competition, 'Have we any humour?' that quality was not the first consideration in awarding the prize.

Herr Naumann is now richer by 100m. not, in the words of the judges, 'because we think that the products of his lively spirits in themselves constitute the essence of humour. We believed rather that his work showed him to be a real man, a man who, as builder's labourer, performs hard physical labour, day in, day out, but who nevertheless employs his short hours of leisure in putting his comic ideas on paper to amuse his comrades.'

'Indiscreet' Comedians

The competition was instituted by the *Angriff* some weeks ago after Dr Goebbels, the Minister of Propaganda, had seen fit to exclude three comedians from the Reich Cultural Chamber, thereby depriving them of their living, for having made indiscreet political jokes. On that occasion Dr Goebbels justified his action in a long newspaper article in which he sought to define humour and to prove that the German people possessed an abundance of that quality while the disgraced comedians did not. The *Angriff* therefore undertook to provide practical proof of the existence of German humour by inviting its readers to send in jokes.

Typical of what does not constitute humour in the eyes of the party is the following joke not current in Berlin:

'. . . exclude three comedians'
[THE MODEL NAZI HUMORIST]

A high official of the Labour Front while visiting a factory saw a workman consuming a large sandwich. 'You know whom you have to thank for that sandwich, don't you?' asked the official. 'You have to thank the leaders of the party.' 'On the contrary,' was the reply, 'I have to thank our accountant, who forgot to deduct the Labour Front dues from my wages this week.'

9 March 1939

'TEA TIMES'

The fact that accents are not usually placed on capital letters in France provided the office of your Paris Correspondent with an unexpected visitor this afternoon. After scanning the plate bearing the words THE TIMES at the entrance a mild-mannered little Frenchman mounted two flights of stairs, entered the office, and, after staring around him in some bewilderment, said, '*Oh, pardon, je croyais que c'etait un thé* (tea room).' Before he could be offered a cup in the spirit of the Entente-Cordiale – which an equally ignorant Englishman once imagined was the name of a liqueur – he departed in apologetic confusion.

1 April 1939

'BILLET DOUX ET CHER'

CANNES A young lawyer of Vienne (Isère), lacking a formal introduction to the object of his affections, sent her a note in a café scribbled on a slip of paper from his pocket indicating a *rendezvous*. On the wireless that evening he heard that his ticket in a State lottery had won 1,000,000f. To his horror, however, he found that his ticket had disappeared, and he then realized that it was on the ticket that he had scribbled his tender appeal. Going to the café the next day he found the lady of his dreams only to be informed that his attentions were unwelcome and that his note had been torn up and thrown away. Later, at the Commissariat of Police, she suggested that any one so stupid had no right to pay any attention to a lady at all. Even the traditional balance of the legal mind broke down before this final thrust, and the young lawyer is at present inconsolable.

1 June 1939

At 11 a.m. on Sunday 3 September 1939 Britain declared war against Germany. On 4 September in the top right-hand corner of the front page of The Times, *above the usual advertisements in letters less than ½-inch high, there appeared the announcement: BRITAIN AT WAR LATEST NEWS.*

NIGHT CLIMB ON THE CATHEDRAL ROOF

Like many other churches, the Cathedral has had its electric light cut off by the local authority as a wartime measure. This makes the climbing of its tower by night none too easy. Two middle-aged air wardens were sent to do it the other night. They were to make sure that no skylight window in the city showed any light.

At 9 o'clock they began their climb, with a verger to guide them who unlocked the great west door and ushered them into the ghostly darkness of the great building. It did not feel asleep, and little noises here and there, a creak and a rustle, made one of the wardens remember a fable of his school days which the headmaster had told on the night he was confirmed, in which the organ and the pews and the stained glass windows were made to talk together in the night, discussing the worth of the batch of candidates who had been confirmed that day.

The climb was by way of a long stone circular staircase, pierced by eyelet windows. They had torches but did not use them. This war has been conducted so far with a commendable absence of spy-mania, but a series of mysterious flashes high up from the eyelet windows of the cathedral might be more than enough to wake lurking suspicions and start a first-class rumour going. Round and round and up and up, with breath getting shorter and shorter. The verger was the oldest of the party and felt it least. It is his duty to conduct parties of visitors up the tower twice every day in the summer, and that night it seemed to his companions that his job was less of a rest-cure than they had previously supposed.

At last there was a pause while the verger fumbled to unlock a door. 'No, we're only halfway yet,' he said, 'but we have to go along above the roof of the cathedral here, and then do the rest of the climb from the other end.' Here a torch was essential. The beams hung so low that to move in the darkness was to ask for concussion. Some bats were fluttering about. They seemed to swoop at the torch's gleam, brushing the hand holding it with their membranes. Bats in the open are harmless, but bats in a building, while no doubt just as harmless, seem much less so. There was real pleasure in reaching the other end, and setting oneself to the circular treadmill once more.

All conversation ceased: there was no breath for it. But just when it seemed that neither legs nor lungs could do more, another door was unlocked, and the verger had us by the arm, guiding us over the ridged lead to the duckboards against the breast-high parapet. The cathedral tower dominates the city and the countryside for miles. There was nothing we could not see except the very thing we had come to look for. No skylights anywhere gleamed and all was clear.

But it was half an hour before we went down, and we did not stay merely to gain our breath. A dark city was spread out below us like a map, but we could not see its contours. Motors, we knew, passed down the main road, but we could not see them. In the fire station and police station lights were blazing as men sat listening and waiting, but they were invisible. We could not even agree as to the place to look for them. Pallid starlight gleamed on a huddle of roofs and chimney pots. We had all known this city for years, two of us for all our lives, but it seemed strange and mysterious and infinitely beautiful. By how gargantuan a madness was it now put in danger in the swift darkness of a summer night!

Yet perhaps the danger was not very great. For there at many points in the fields and heaths below us searchlights patterned the dark sky with their restless bars of light, and to every one there was a gun somewhere not far away manned by Territorials following every movement of the light. Suddenly the silence was broken. The deep coughing of a fog horn, which the engines of a certain railway seem to think are whistles, was heard, and a long train swept round a gradual curve and roared through the station. The windows of the coaches were darkened, but there was no ARP about the two engines. Great beacons of flaming light streamed backwards from their open fire-boxes, and even from that height we could see the tiny figure of a fireman in the leading engine rhythmically bending and swaying as he reached a shovel-full of coal from the tender and thrust it into the furnace. Again and again he did it, a poetic grace of economy in the swing of his body and arms, until the train ran behind a hill and we could see him no more.

Then we turned and stumped our blind way down again. We had seen no skylights, and our legs ached again, but it had been worth it.

13 September 1939

CHRISTMAS AT THE FRONT

ON THE WESTERN FRONT Bitter cold fell on the British units facing the enemy on the Franco-German frontier at Christmas. The shallower ponds and rivulets were frozen solid, and the surface of the earth was hardened into an ice-bound crust. Patches of mist hung low over the watercourses, and the rumble of gunfire echoed far through the soft winter air. Sometimes the deep thud of the guns was punctuated by the muffled 'toc-toc-toc' of automatic weapons, but it was difficult to say whether they were in action or practising in some disused quarry. On Christmas Day itself not a shot was fired.

Sometimes a violent duel would break out between the French guns sunk deep in the great forts of the Maginot Line and the light guns of the enemy, but undisturbed by these sudden gusts of anger, the British troops are consolidating the area which has been allotted to them. British outposts stand guard in front of the chain of brooding fortresses that form the Maginot Line. British reserve positions are manned behind it. The troops are quartered in empty villages, some of which were evacuated in confusion at two hours' notice. Billets are less comfortable here than in the area occupied by the main body of the BEF,* but the men have a better climate and

* British Expeditionary Force

more emotional stimulus to sustain them.

The turkeys and plum puddings sent out for Christmas were eaten in log huts buried deep in the woods. Here some of the outposts are situated. They are not allowed to have fires since the smoke might guide enemy patrols. From these crude huts the men steal out across No Man's Land at night on their dangerous errands.

At first it appears that the line is thinly held. You can travel for miles without seeing troops gathered thickly on the ground. Only after moving from the most rearward reserved position through supplementary lines to the point where further road traffic is discouraged, and from there looking to the dim distance where the eye can just make out the contours of crests patrolled by British advance guards, can you grasp the great depth of the defensive system and visualize the murderous concentration of force that could be brought against the flanks and rear of an attacker who dared to penetrate the forward area.

27 December 1939

RIDING PILLION ON A SPITFIRE

A young aircraftman at a Royal Air Force fighter command station has the distinction of having 'ridden' a Spitfire 'bareback'. He is a rigger, and was finishing off a job on the tail of a Spitfire. He was sitting astride the fuselage facing tailwards, and the engine was running. The pilot, unaware that the rigger was still on the tail, took off.

Puzzled by the weight and the unresponsive behaviour of his aircraft, the pilot made a circuit of the aerodrome, while his passenger gripped tight with knees and arms. After a second circuit the pilot landed smoothly. The medical officer hurried across, but the aircraftman was found to be none the worse. He has even offered to repeat the ride for a £5 bet, but there are no takers.

29 March 1940

QUISLING IS AS QUISLING DOES

We should all be profoundly grateful to Major Quisling. He has added a new word to the English language. Before the Nazi invasion of Norway he was virtually unheard of in this country, though a few readers with peculiarly tenacious memories may have recalled that just over eight years ago an attempt was made on his life with knives and pepper. During the past week, however, he has attained a swift notoriety. Not only has his name been heard or read by almost everybody, but twice already it has been used in these columns as a plain synonym for 'traitor'. Last Friday Sweden was described as being 'on the watch for possible Quislings'; and on Tuesday it was wisely stated that there were 'Quislings in every country in Europe'.

To journalists and other writers, weary of racking their brains or raking the well-thumbed pages of Roget in search of alternatives, the word 'Quisling' is a gift from the gods. If they had been ordered to invent a new word for 'traitor' and given *carte blanche* with the alphabet, they could hardly have hit upon a more brilliant combination of letters. Aurally, it contrives to suggest something at once slippery and tortuous. Visually, it has the supreme merit of beginning with a 'Q', which (with one august exception) has long seemed to the British mind to be a crooked, uncertain, and slightly disreputable letter, suggestive of the questionable, the querulous, the quavering, of quaking quagmires and quivering quicksands, of quibbles and quarrels, of queasiness, quackery, qualms, and Quilp.

Quisling, then, be it. We welcome the word as sincerely as we detest the qualities which it connotes.

19 April 1940

AN AIRMAN TO HIS MOTHER

Among the personal belongings of a young RAF pilot in a Bomber Squadron who was recently reported 'Missing,

'. . . beginning with a 'Q'
[QUISLING IS AS QUISLING DOES]

believed killed', was a letter to his mother – to be sent to her if he were killed.

'This letter was perhaps the most amazing one I have ever read; simple and direct in its wording but splendid and uplifting in its outlook,' says the young officer's station commander. 'It was inevitable that I should read it – in fact he must have intended this, for it was left open in order that I might be certain that no prohibited information was disclosed.

'I sent the letter to the bereaved mother, and asked her whether I might publish it anonymously, as I feel its contents may bring comfort to other mothers, and that every one in our country may feel proud to read of the sentiments which support "an average airman" in the execution of his present arduous duties. I have received the mother's permission, and I hope this letter may be read by the greatest possible number of our countrymen at home and abroad.'

Text of the Letter

Dearest Mother, – Though I feel no premonition at all, events are moving rapidly, and I have instructed that this letter be forwarded to you should I fail to return from one of the raids which we shall shortly be called upon to undertake. You must hope on for a month, but at the end of that time you must accept the fact that I have handed my task over to the extremely capable hands of my comrades of the Royal Air Force, as so many splendid fellows have already done.

First, it will comfort you to know that my role in this war has been of the greatest importance. Our patrols far out over the North Sea have helped to keep the trade routes clear for our convoys and supply ships, and on one occasion our information was instrumental in saving the lives of the men in a crippled lighthouse relief ship. Though it will be difficult for you, you will disappoint me if you do not at least try to accept the facts dispassionately, for I shall have done my duty to the utmost of my ability.

No man can do more, and no one calling himself a man could do less.

I have always admired your amazing courage in the face of continual setbacks; in the way you have given me as good an education and background as anyone in the country; and always kept up appearances without ever losing faith in the future. My death would not mean that your struggle has been in vain. Far from it. It means that your sacrifice is as great as mine. Those who serve England must expect nothing from her; we debase ourselves if we regard our country as merely a place in which to eat and sleep.

History resounds with illustrious names who have given all, yet their sacrifice has resulted in the British Empire, where there is a measure of peace, justice, and freedom for all, and where a higher standard of civilization has evolved, and is still evolving, than anywhere else. But this is not only concerning our own land. Today we are faced with the greatest organized challenge to Christianity and civilization that the world has ever seen, and I count myself lucky and honoured to be the right age and fully trained to throw my full weight into the scale. For this I have to thank you. Yet there is more work for you to do. The home front will still have to stand united for years after the war is won. For all that can be said against it, I still maintain that this war is a very good thing; every individual is having the chance to give and dare all for his principle like the martyrs of old. However long the time may be, one thing can never be altered – I shall have lived and died an Englishman. Nothing else matters one jot nor can anything ever change it.

You must not grieve for me, for if you really believe in religion and all that it entails that would be hypocrisy. I have no fear of death; only a queer elation . . . I would have it no other way. The universe is so vast and so ageless that the life of one man can only be justified by the measure of his sacrifice. We are sent to this world to acquire a personality and a character to take with us that can never be taken from us. Those who just eat and sleep, prosper and procreate, are no better than animals if all their lives they are at peace.

I firmly and absolutely believe that evil things are sent into the world to try us; they are sent deliberately by our Creator to test our metal because He knows what is good for us. The Bible is full of cases where the easy way out has been discarded for moral principles.

I count myself fortunate in that I have seen the whole country and known men of every calling. But with the final test of war I consider my character fully developed. Thus at my early age my earthly mission is already fulfilled and I am prepared to die with just one regret, and one only, that I could not devote myself to making your declining years more happy by being with you; but you will live in peace and freedom and I shall have directly contributed to that, so here again my life will not have been in vain.

Your loving Son,

18 June 1940

[This letter was reprinted in several forms and widely circulated during the war years.]

'I HAVE STOMACH ACHE'

Phrase books in English and German have been issued to the German Army, containing questions which German troops would be likely to put to English citizens if they succeeded in achieving their desire to overrun the country. Some of these books have come into the hands of the British military authorities. Throughout there is a warning that if you fail to tell their soldiers the truth you will be shot.

Some of the questions in the phrase book are apparently designed for use in cross-examining civic leaders. The question 'Are you the mayor?' is followed by the demand 'Open all cupboards' and 'Where is the cash?' The handbook then 'instructs' the Nazi soldier how to ask the mayor to write down the amount which is in the safe and to find out if there is any more money in the building. Should he succeed in obtaining information he would then use the phrase 'I confiscate all this money.' Also, if he follows his handbook, he would tell the mayor that if he lies he will be shot.

A whole section consists of questions intended to enable the German troops to find their way about the country. In this case citizens will be assured that 'If you tell the truth you have nothing to fear.'

The authors of the handbook do not appear to have overlooked any contingency. There are even such phrases as 'I have the stomach ache,' 'Give me opium,' or 'Give me pills.'

The Germans obviously intend to have clean linen, for they are instructed how to demand from the people on whom they thrust themselves for board and lodgings that they shall wash two shirts, one pair of pants, and three pocket handkerchiefs. There are instructions about everything – from medicine to horses and carts. Drivers are warned that if they intentionally take the wrong turning they will be shot.

The booklet is similar to those which Germany has produced in Czech, Polish, and Russian languages.

25 June 1940

53 RAIDERS SHOT DOWN IN CHANNEL

In the biggest air battle fought since the evacuation from Dunkirk, the RAF yesterday shot down 53 enemy aircraft in the English Channel. Sixteen of our fighter pilots are reported missing.

German air attacks on a convoy were made at intervals throughout the day, and were preceded before dawn by an attack by motor torpedo-boats ('E' boats). Three coastal vessels in the convoy were torpedoed and sunk; one 'E' boat was sunk and another was damaged.

. . . The day's main air battle was fought in three parts. The first German attack on a convoy took place between 9 and 9.30 in the morning when six Junkers 87 dive-bombers and three Messerschmitts were destroyed by the Hurricane squadron which was most successful on the day's engagements.

A second attack on the same convoy by a still larger formation of dive-bombers, escorted by fighters, developed between 11.30 a.m. and 1 p.m. Finally, throwing nearly 150 dive-bombers and fighters into the battle, the Germans made a third attack between 4 and 5 p.m.

The Hurricane squadron which destroyed 21 German raiders was in all three actions. In a few hours they became the squadron with the biggest 'bag' of enemy aircraft in the home defence. Their squadron leader, describing one of the fights, said that the sky over the convoy was 'literally black' with German bombers and fighters.

A Pole's Victim

After the first morning battle the Polish flying officer, who speaks very little English, told, with the help of his fellow-pilots, how he saw his first large formation of Junkers 87's supported by the new Heinkel 113 fighters.

'I was attacked,' he said, 'by three Heinkel 113's, who seemed to be working to a plan. One was flying alone and the other two as a pair. If you attack the pair the single one tries to get on your tail.'

He tackled the single Heinkel 113 and watched it go down smoking, though he was not able to see the final crash. The other two flew off. It was during the last battle of the afternoon that this Polish pilot got his first Messerschmitt 109.

Here is a description of the first action today by the squadron leader of the most successful Hurricane squadron.

'We climbed to 16,000 ft,' he said, 'and, looking down, saw a large formation of Junkers 87's approaching from the south, with Messerschmitt 109's stepped up behind to 20,000 ft. We approached unobserved out of the sun and went in to attack the rear Junkers 87's before the enemy fighters could interfere.

'I gave a five-seconds burst to one bomber and broke off to engage two Messerschmitt 109's. There was a dog fight. The enemy fighters, who were painted silver, were half rolling and diving and zooming in climbing turns. I fired two five-seconds bursts at one and saw it dive into the sea. Then I followed another up in a zoom and got him as he stalled.'

A flight lieutenant in the same squadron managed to bring down two Junkers 87's, though his engines had stopped.

'I was forced to retire owing to engine failure, but dived down on a Junkers 87,' he said. 'After a three- or four-seconds burst it went into an inverted dive and crashed into the sea. My engine started again, so I went after another Junkers 87 and attacked him before he was able to make his dive-bombing attack on the convoy. He dived into the sea at high speed. After this second attack my engine stopped for good and I only just got back to England.'

He managed to reach an aerodrome.

In the second battle of the day three Hurricanes of this squadron met 10 Messerschmitt 110's and shot three of them and a Messerschmitt 109 down into the sea. The Messerschmitt 109 was being used as a decoy. While the Hurricanes were tackling it the Messerschmitt 110's were supposed to take them by surprise. But as one of the Hurricane pilots said, 'The Messerschmitt 109 overacted his part.'

While this part of the battle was going on, a Spitfire squadron was carrying the fight over to the French coast. They chased seven Messerschmitt 109's over the Channel and destroyed six of them. Then as a finishing touch one of them fired at a German motor torpedo boat off Calais. 'Several of the crew fell overboard,' he said.

The pilot of one of the British fighters that was lost, by his last act prevented his burning machine from falling in the centre of a South-East Coast town. With black smoke pouring from it, the fighter burst into flames and, blazing from stem to stern, looked as though it must inevitably crash into some buildings. He was rapidly losing height, but the pilot remained at his controls until the machine dived into the sea 50 yards from the shore. Motor-boats went to the spot, but found no trace of the pilot's body.

9 August 1940

[The Battle of Britain]

CONSCIENCE MONEY AFTER 39 YEARS

Two annas (about 2¼d) has been sent to the Secretary of the Railway Board of the Government of India as conscience money, which has preyed on the mind of the sender for 39 years. It was sent by money order, costing the sender another 2 annas, and it was accompanied by this letter:

I beg to say that at the time of the Delhi Durbar, held in 1901, I was at Kingsway; it was very cold; I could not stay there; there was nothing in my pocket, so I travelled without a ticket. There was a great rush, so I could not be checked, but my conscience has been checking me for so many years. To satisfy my conscience, and to remove the pressure on my mind, I send you the money due; I can pay you any penalty you suggest. I hope you will kindly receive the little sum and oblige.

4 October 1940

[Up until a few years after the end of the Second World War, announcements occasionally appeared in *The Times*, headed 'Conscience Money'. It would be reported that the Chancellor of the Exchequer acknowledged the receipt of this or that sum from XYZ or ABC. This, according to an editorial, would 'rouse in minds naturally suspicious a little wonder whether XYZ or ABC was not trying to have it both ways. He had enjoyed the use of the money that he had withheld; and he might now enjoy the glow of conscious virtue in making reparation, see his noble deed (though he alone would know it was his) published to the world in *The Times*, and still avoid open confession or the incitement of the Treasury to keep a sharp eye on him for the future.' Anything so hypocritical would of course be unthinkable to the honest tax-payer of the 1980s.]

FAREWELL TO SILK STOCKINGS

Almost the first public act of the new President of the Board of Trade has been to announce that the home sale of silk hosiery will be prohibited after next month. In ordinary times this would not be a promising way of starting a political career: but at such a time as this even silk stockings and the rest will be sacrificed, if not gladly, at least without serious protest – and there is always artificial silk.

Artificial silk is not included in the prohibition and this, it seems, in the view of the wearers of silk stockings, is much to be thankful for. As one woman put it, while 'pure silk is nicer', artificial silk is 'bearable'. Incidentally, silk stockings fill all the headlines; not a word is said about silk socks. Yet men, too, will have to make the sacrifice; nor will silk underwear be available to them. For, although the matter is rather obscure, it seems that hosiery as defined by the Board of Trade includes underwear. It may even include some other garments made of silk.

One thing is certain. As real silk is wanted for the manufacture of barrage balloons, parachutes, and other essentials of the day, there will be no more pure silk stockings in the shops after November 30. Stocks remaining – and all who can are likely to lay in extra stockings and underwear – will be diverted to overseas markets. Many women normally wear artificial silk, but as a luxury hose for special occasions pure silk stockings are popular.

Thousands of women have already given up stockings, silk or artificial silk. Many, usually those employed in the civil defence services, have taken to the regular wearing of 'slacks'.

There are already on the market fancy weave wool stockings which may be accepted as a substitute for silk.

21 October 1940

THE ANSWER WAS AN ONION

A Coastal Command Sunderland flying-boat picked up a convoy far out at sea, and no soooner had it taken up its station than a ship at the tail of the steaming line began to signal by lamp. The word 'onions' was spelt out in Morse several times – just that one word.

The code book gave no possible explanation, and the Sunderland signalled: 'Message not understood. Please repeat and explain.' Still the merchant ship continued to signal 'Onions', so the flying-boat captain gave it up and flew on to watch for submarines.

A fortnight later the flying-boat crew received a letter from the skipper of the ship. It was addressed to the flying-boat under its identification letters, 'c/o Air Ministry, London'.

This is what the letter said: 'We had been listening to the wireless news and heard that you in England were suffering from an acute shortage of onions. My ship was loaded with onions, and I wanted to give the good news to the first bit of England we sighted, and you were it.'

Another ship in the convoy had a strange, white-bearded figure hoisted at the mast-head. An exchange of Morse signals showed that the ship had a cargo of fruit for the Christmas markets and had thought it appropriate to have a Father Christmas figurehead.

22 November 1940

SODA WATER SYPHONS AS FIRE PUMPS

Readers of *The Times* in many parts of the country continue to send suggestions which are in the main related to various aspects of the national war effort.

The Rev. E. G. Drummond writes from Oxford that 'the suggestion of making a soda water syphon serve as a substitute for a stirrup pump may be much improved by using a gas pipe connexion of rubber. One end is put on the tube of the syphon and the other end on a vulcanite mouthpiece of a tobacco pipe. The jet will then become a fine spray, which can be aimed in any direction with increased efficiency'.

5 February 1941

'. . . substitute for a stirrup pump'
[SODA WATER SYPHONS AS FIRE PUMPS]

LOVE BY NUMBERS

War, as is well known, spawns initials with uncontrollable fecundity; in the last conflict they burst the bounds of the official communications of Dados and the GOC-in-C, and overflowed into the private correspondence of the PBI and even of QAIMNSVR. The junior officer who had to censor the letters of his men soon learnt to recognize such phrases as CYK, which admonished the recipient to consider herself kissed, and THF, which, even though an industrious correspondent sometimes used it to close simultaneous letters to several different ladies, guaranteed his fidelity till Hell should freeze. If the censor was a conscientious man, he paused before licking down the flap to see whether any special trust was imposed on him by its being inscribed SWALK, which meant that it was to be sealed with a loving kiss.

But it seems that the troops of today require such epistolary endearments to be still further abbreviated. This may result from the accelerated pace of modern war; or perhaps it has been rendered necessary because the three Services have at last come near to exhausting all the possible permutations of the alphabet. The initials FLAK, for instance, have been appropriated by the Royal Air Force to convey a shade of meaning distinctly different from 'fondest love and kisses'; so, lest the latter phrase should be consequently lost to the private vocabulary of the fighting man, the ingenious Sir Edward Wilshaw, chairman of Cable and Wireless, offers him an alternative abbreviation. He represents this affectionate message by the simple number 44, and includes it in a series of thirty-eight possible greetings, each of which can be numerically condensed in like manner. Thus the soldier has only to pick from the list the number representing the precise degree of benevolence or passion that he feels, and the Postmaster-General – who has enthusiastically adopted Sir Edward's idea – will convey his sentiments telegraphically at the minimum of expense.

The list, it is understood, has been made out after

exhaustive statistical analysis of the messages actually transmitted by Cable and Wireless, whose vast experience enables them to gauge and tabulate with minute precision all the standard feelings that may blossom in the military heart. Thus greeting forty-four, which has already been quoted, is itself the superlative of a nicely graduated scale, of which the positive is forty-two, 'kisses', and the comparative forty-three, 'love and kisses'. 'All my love' is carefully differentiated from 'all our love' and from the reckless 'all my love dearest'; and 'birthday greetings' may be sent plain or loving according to taste and without extra charge. The list may even serve the soldier as something more than a manual of correspondence; properly used, it will help him in the planning of his life. Hitherto no doubt he has relied on the rough-and-ready method of pulling alternate petals off a daisy, or counting plum-stones to the tune of 'she loves me, she loves me not'. These were good enough for the unscientific age; but today it is advisable to use Sir Edward Wilshaw's mathematically coordinated scale as an emotional thermometer.

Let the soldier then examine his conscience and ask himself what number honestly represents the message he would instinctively send to the girl he left behind him when he embarked for active service. If his temperature is twenty-seven, which stands for 'loving greetings', his feeling is probably no more than fraternal. Forty-three, or even forty-two, the significance of which has been already explained, is sufficiently promising for some merry dalliance on seven days' leave. Fifty-six – 'my thoughts are with you' – might justify a field officer in contemplating a mature and rational alliance. But the younger man should not be content with anything less than thirty-five – 'fondest love darling' – as the basis of a lifelong partnership.

1 March 1941

WHERE NOT TO KEEP YOUR BANK BOOK

Broadcasting last night on the importance of saving, Mr L. Simon, director of Savings and Controller of the Post Office Savings bank, advised people to keep a separate record of the number of their bank book and the amount of the balance.

'Do not go near an elephant with your book in your pocket,' he said, 'and don't let your wife use your book to singe a fowl.' These tips are based on actual experience.

'Do not keep your book in an oven. If you hide it away for safe keeping remember where you put it. You may not be as lucky as the woman who found her missing book in an old piece of music called "God send you back to me".'

Many people who might help the country and keep the money safe by putting it in the Savings Bank were keeping it at home exposed to the hazards of civilian life. One man killed in a recent raid had £800 in his pockets, and in a demolished house charred notes worth £400 were found.

22 April 1941

DISGUISED LAMPOON OF HITLER

The following poem, apparently in praise of Hitler, was recently published in the Nazi newspaper *Paris-Soir*, as a contribution from an anonymous reader:

Aimons et admirons le Chancelier Hitler
L' eternelle Angleterre est indigne de vivre.
Maudissons, écrasons le peuple d'outre mer;
Le Nazi sur le terre sera seul à survivre.
Soyons donc le soutien du Führer allemand,
Des boys navigateurs finira l'odyssée;
À eux seuls appartient un juste châtiment;
La palme du vainqueur attend la Croix Gammée.

France, the Free French newspaper published in London, which has reproduced these lines, points out, however, that the Germans have been imposed upon by a practical joker, and that the real meaning appears when the poem is divided longitudinally into two verses, as follows:

Aimons et admirons	Le Chancelier Hitler
L'eternelle Angleterre	Est indigne de vivre.
Maudissons, écrasons	Le peuple d'outre mer
Le Nazi sur la terre.	Sera seul à survivre.
Soyons donc le soutien	Du Führer allemand
Des boys navigateurs:	Finira l'odyssée:
À eux seuls appartient	Un juste châtiment
La palme du vainqueur.	Attend la Croix Gammée.

25 April 1941

BOMBER SAVED BY SHEILA'S 'LOVE AND KISSES'

The story of a girl's message of good wishes that saved an RAF bomber and its crew of four was told by Mr Attlee, Lord Privy Seal, in a speech at Norwich last night.

The bomber, he said, had to fly through a lot of flak over Germany and one of its wings was damaged. On the homeward journey the fabric began to come away from the wing, but the tearing suddenly stopped.

The pilot made a safe landing and then found that the stoppage of the tear was caused by some extremely careful stitching of the fabric. Removal of this disclosed a message: 'To the airman who will fly this plane. All good wishes, love and kisses from Sheila.'

Sheila was discovered, added Mr Attlee, and the pilot showed her the message. When she admitted that she was the writer, he told her she had saved his life and added: 'Now I have come for my kisses.'

13 October 1941

GERMAN AEROPLANE'S STICKY END

A German aircraft was recently shot down by German anti-aircraft fire aimed at British bombers on their way to the Rhineland. In the early morning hours a couple of Dutch painters from a neighbouring town were ordered to cover up the German markings on the wrecked aeroplane with those of the RAF. The painters did their work, with obvious reluctance, but thought of a clever way to spoil the German game. They left a prominently displayed notice: 'Wet paint'.

28 October 1941

MR CHURCHILL'S PISTOL

Mr Brendan Bracken, Minister of Information, told his constituents in Paddington the following story of the Prime Minister:

Mr Churchill was about to leave by aeroplane for the last journey to France. As we walked down the stairs together, with the rain pelting down outside, he looked extremely grave. Suddenly he turned to his butler and said: 'Get my heavy pistol for me.' I asked him why he wanted it. 'Well,' replied the Prime Minister, 'if we are attacked by the enemy, I may be able to account for at least one German.'

19 November 1941

MARRIAGE TO A DEAD GERMAN SOLDIER

The *Münchener Neueste Nachrichten* reports that existing German laws provide that a marriage may be solemnized even though the man has been killed in the war, if his intention to wed the woman to whom he was betrothed was clearly expressed beforehand. It cites the case of Lieutenant Fritz Storch, who declared before witnesses on

17 October 1941 that he intended to marry, but who delayed the wedding and was later killed.

The marriage has just been solemnized at Schönigen. The place before the registrar where the bridegroom would normally stand was occupied by a rosette of crêpe and a helmet and sword, as symbols that the bridegroom had fallen in the defence of the fatherland.

16 April 1942

'MONTH OF POLITENESS' FOR GERMANS

The German authorities in Berlin have proclaimed that May must be a 'month of politeness', during which every one must be encouraged to be polite to his fellow-Germans. This is not always the case at present. The appeal makes special reference to tram conductors, shop assistants, and the general shopping public.

To give concrete reality to the idea, a special organization of umpires has been formed to award prizes to individuals who are judged to have been most successful in this 'politeness competition', which is designed to restore 'gladness, kindness, and courtesy' to Germany. The first prize will be of 1,000 marks; the second a gramophone; and the third, 10 theatre tickets.

The Nazi newspaper *Das Schwarze Korps* demands that all Jews should be compelled to wear bowler hats, because, it is stated, they are tending more and more to 'disguise' themselves as German workers, and a Jew is often unrecognizable from a back view.

17 April 1942

THE STICKIEST JOB

The salvage of foodstuffs damaged by enemy action still continues. Of the total quantity of foodstuffs damaged in this country by air raids up to the end of last year, nearly three-quarters has been saved.

A representative of the Ministry of Food said yesterday that in view of the appeals made to the public to economize in food it should be emphasized that, so far as bulk stocks were concerned, the country had been extremely fortunate in saving food from destruction. The exact figure of stock thus saved was 73.7 per cent.

One of the best examples of salvage is a very large stock of sugar. The sheds in which the sugar was stored were hit by enemy action and burned to the ground. The sugar was in the basement. Salvage officers immediately called in sugar experts, who gave the opinion that the work of salvage would be well worth doing. This work still goes on.

'It is probably the stickiest job that men could be put to,' said the Ministry representative. 'When it rains a certain amount of sugar is immediately converted into treacle. Nevertheless the work is going on and when the treacle or sugar is refined extremely little of it has to be discarded.'

22 April 1942

A LEGACY OF ASHES

A rich peasant of Vila Boim, Portugal, knowing that 'you can't take it with you', and mistrusting the use to which his relatives might put the sum in banknotes which he had saved, burned it all an hour before he died, leaving only, in a prominent position on the mantelpiece, the equivalent of a £10 note to pay for his funeral.

4 May 1942

'FOR GERMANS ONLY' – PROPHECY ON WARSAW LAMP-POSTS

News from Poland records that the authorities in Warsaw

were embarrassed for several days during the first half of May by finding written on many lamp-posts during the night in unremovable paint, 'Nur für Deutsche' (for Germans only) – the inscription which Germans display outside the best restaurants, hotels, gardens, and the like where Poles and Jews are not allowed.

It may be recalled that some time ago a number of 'Nur für Deutsche' notices were secretly removed from their customary places and displayed at the entrances to Warsaw cemeteries.

19 May 1942

TREASURES AMONG SALVAGE

The need for careful examination of salvage is emphasized by the discovery of a bronze statuette of 'Venus after the Bath', designed by Giovanni Bologna (1524–1608), which came to light recently among a quantity of old metal collected by the Hampstead salvage organization. It was picked out by Mr James Mann, Keeper of the Wallace Collection, who was asked to look over a number of objects in case there should be anything of artistic value among them.

Giovanni Bologna was born at Douai, and later took the name by which he became famous after the town of Boulogne-sur-Mer. In 1554 he went to Rome and in 1556 to Florence, eventually becoming more Italian than the Italians. He entered the service of the Medici family, in which he remained until his death, and brought about a revival of Italian sculpture. His work has never gone out of fashion, and statues after his models have continued to be produced down to the present.

The statuette which has now been discovered is probably not from his own hand but a fine seventeenth or eighteenth century example. It is admirably finished, with a good patina, and is to figure in a forthcoming Red Cross sale. The sculptor's original of this subject is almost certainly the signed example which was presented in 1565 by Cosimo dei Medici to the Emperor Maximilian II, now at Vienna.

5 June 1942

COUPONS FOR ARTISTS' CANVAS

Complaint has been made by artists that under the clothes' rationing scheme they are compelled to give up dress coupons in order to get canvas on which to paint their pictures. This disability, they point out, cannot have been intended when the rationing of clothing materials was introduced. It is understood that the matter is being considered by the Board of Trade.

10 June 1942

WAR-TIME RECIPE – NO. 11

A good travelling alternative to a sandwich, the spiced meat round served to passengers in British Overseas Aircraft is easy to make and also good coupon value. Put the contents of a tin of pork sausage meat into a basin, first removing the jelly. Mix the meat and fat thoroughly together, add a pinch of herbs, if liked. Add 1 lb self-raising flour and rub into the meat gently with the tips of the fingers. Add cold water to the jelly to make up to 7 oz., with a good pinch of salt. Mix this thoroughly into the paste. Roll out just over ½ in. thick, cut into 4 in. rounds, glaze with processed egg dissolved in water, bake in a very hot oven. Split when cold and fill with sliced cucumber, tomato, raw cabbage, or any filling, or eat plain. This is sufficient for 20 portions.

14 August 1942

[Probably the nastiest recipe ever published in *The Times*.]

'. . . to paint their pictures'
[COUPONS FOR ARTISTS' CANVAS]

'YOU'VE HAD IT!'

A soldier, required the other day to supply his seniors with the piece of slang most likely to have been given lasting currency by the modern Army, answered a little ruefully: 'You've had it!' The implication was that the boys in light blue had stolen a march on the men in khaki, and that to the Air Force belongs the credit of sponsoring the only service phrase as yet deserving to rank with 'San Fairy Ann', that catch-as-catch-can adaptation reckoned by members of the Home Guard the chief linguistic achievement of their youth. The soldier's evidence is not, of course, conclusive. Somewhat surprisingly the dialogue of *Flare Path*, which brought the expression to the stage last week, made room for an explanatory footnote. Was this, it may be wondered, modesty in the dramatist – Mr Terence Rattigan is himself a member of the Air Force – or is there faintheartedness among the sponsors? But they cannot, surely, believe that there are today among the tolerably well informed some who do not know the phrase for what it is, an ironic form of refusal ready to the tongue for all and sundry who are very properly asked for something which they cannot possibly or even conveniently give. A more likely reason for the footnote is that while the many-pointed irony has already broken out of air stations into common understanding it has still to pass into common use and that Mr Rattigan deemed it expedient to dwell upon its usefulness and beauty.

Whether the locution is worthy of a place among the logical anomalies of English idiom philologists must determine, and film critics can say if it comes from America, the home of harshly ironic turns of speech. Lesser folk, considering its fitness for daily use, may think that it has a good prospect of establishing itself, at least for the duration of the war. The war has turned this into the most inconvenient of all possible worlds, and as the manufacture of one thing after another falls under prohibition the inconvenienced are unlikely to hit upon a more recurringly apt comment than the dryly succinct

'You've had it!' It would have gladdened William Morris, who long ago maintained that many of the things we are losing now were useless and only produced by diverting labour from properly creative ends. 'The most of these things,' he wrote of goods displayed in London shop windows, 'no one, serious or unserious, wants at all; only a foolish habit makes even the lightest-minded of us suppose that he wants them; and to many people, even of those who buy them, they are obvious encumbrances to real work, thought, and pleasure.' Whether we agree or disagree with Morris as to what constituted a waste of labour, his words are consolatory at a time when hard necessity has played havoc with possible superfluities. It is difficult to carry Morris's eloquently and acutely argued consolation in mind, much as it might fortify the foolish heart against deprivations yet to come, but 'You've had it!' has a rough eloquence of its own and is easy to remember. Harsh it may be in its utter finality, in its brisk acceptance of the inevitable, but its very brevity is bracing, and it consorts well with that other phrase of contemporary and civilian coinage: 'We can take it!'

19 August 1942

PENICILLIUM

Some thirteen years ago the discovery was made that a mould, *Penicillium Notatum*, possessed strong anti-bacterial powers. Study of the mould was continued in Oxford and the further discovery achieved that purified preparations are much more richly endowed with bactericidal properties than is the crude substance. A preparation of *penicillium* has been found to inhibit the growth of staphylococci completely in a dilution of 1 in 25,000,000 and partially in a dilution of 1 in 160,000,000. An additional advantage is the harmlessness of the drug. In experiments on mice no ill effects were observed, though very large dosees were given, and doses given to human beings seemed to be innocuous. Thus the hope emerges that it may be possible to produce and maintain in the blood a sufficient concentration to bring some at least of the organisms of disease under therapeutic control. The prospect is certainly an alluring one, especially when it is borne in mind that penicillin is many hundred times as active as the sulphonamides which, in recent years, have so largely dominated the field of treatment.

Pencillin has, in fact, been found to be active against certain organisms which have resisted the influence of the sulphonamides. Such activity may very well constitute its most important quality, because, as things stand at present, organisms resistant to the sulphonamides are, for the most part, beyond the reach of treatment. In any case penicillin is less toxic than the least toxic of the sulphonamides and seems to act without reference to the number of bacteria present. Efforts are now being made to obtain the active principle of the drug in crystalline form since – as the *Lancet*, which recently discussed the subject fully, points out – it is not yet certain that the maximum degree of purity has been achieved. There are, however, many difficulties in the way and further hopes of obtaining a synthetic product are not very bright. This is perhaps immaterial seeing that the mould itself is available. There will be general agreement with the plea of the *Lancet* that, 'in view of its potentialities, methods for producing penicillin on a large scale should be developed as quickly as possible'.

27 August 1942

[A few days after this article appeared *The Times* printed a letter from Sir Almroth E. Wright, pointing out that 'on the principle *Palmam qui meruit ferat*, the laurel wreath for this discovery should be put on the brow of Professor Alexander Fleming, of the Inoculation Department of St Mary's Hospital, Paddington'.]

THE TEMPTER IN A RESTAURANT

Major Thesiger told Chelsea Borough Council on Wednesday night this story: After lunching at a Chelsea restaurant a man tried to persuade the proprietor to serve him with an extra course 'off the ration'. The proprietor firmly refused, saying: 'You know you have inspector written all over you.' The man replied: 'You are right. I am a Ministry of Food Inspector. How did you know?' Major Thesiger said he thought such conduct on the part of officials was damnable. 'I don't think that in order to get convictions people should be tempted into crime,' he added. 'Those are the methods that prevail in Germany.'

28 August 1942

'AUSTERITY' BALLET DANCERS

According to the *Australian Newsletter*, issued from Australia House, the manager of a Sydney theatre who applied to the Department of Labour this week for permission to employ 40 women as ballet dancers, was told that they must be over 45 years of age. The manager's reply was not disclosed, but the Deputy Director-General of Man-power said that it was not proposed to permit young women to do that class of work, as their services were needed for war work.

17 September 1942

THE WORLD HEARS BRITAIN'S BELLS

A pleasant noise of bells broke out yesterday morning over the kingdom to celebrate – in the words issued from Downing Street – 'the success granted to the forces of the Empire and our allies in the Battle of Egypt and as a call to thanksgiving and to renewed prayer'.

The bells were also heard over a large part of the world,

'. . . over 45 years of age'
['AUSTERITY' BALLET DANCERS]

for the BBC broadcast peals and chimes in a mid-morning programme reaching North and South America, the Pacific, allied countries, occupied Europe, and Germany. Those world-wide audiences heard the bells of Westminster Abbey, of St Cuthbert's, Edinburgh, of Armagh and Landaff Cathedrals, of a village church at Prestwich, Lancashire, and finally of Coventry Cathedral. The announcer asked the secret listeners on the Continent: 'Did you hear them in occupied Europe? Did you hear them in Germany? After noon to-day they will be silent again, except for warning of invasion if needed, till they ring out for final victory.'

Two Years' Silence

The bells of St Paul's were rung for the first time since the outbreak of war. For Canterbury and other cathedrals and churches it was the first time since the Government imposed its ban on the ringing of church bells in June, 1940. Many of the churches in the City, as elsewhere, could not ring their bells because of destruction or damage from the air raids, or because the bells have been moved to safety.

It was possible to ring only eight of the 13 bells of bomb-scarred Exeter Cathedral . . . At Portsmouth the Pompey chimes, known to sailors all over the world, were rung by hand from the tower of the raid-damaged Guildhall. For half an hour yesterday morning 14 volunteers, having climbed the ruined tower, worked the striking hammers of the bells by hand, and ended by striking the noon hour in the same way.

Ancient Societies

It was a big day for the societies of bellringers, some of whose members must have fretted for long under the necessity of refraining from the practice of their hobby and mystery. The Ancient Society of College Youths rang the bells of St Paul's, as they have done since the cathedral was built. With volunteers from other churches they rang two touches of Stedman cinques with a short interval between, and then went off to ring peals at Stepney Parish Church. Similarly the Royal Cumberland Youths, besides ringing chimes at St Martin-in-the-Fields, their headquarters, lent a hand at other London churches during the morning. At Westminster Abbey 504 changes of Stedman triples were rung by another band of College Youths, whose conductor at the treble bell was Mr H. R. Newton, aged 77, and a bellringer for 58 years.

16 November 1942

[The ban on the ringing of church bells 'except as a signal of an enemy attack' had been imposed on 13 June 1940. It was not finally lifted until May 1943.]

STUBBORN RESISTANCE

The Caucasian army continues its pursuit of the enemy along the trans-Caucasian railway towards Mineralniye Vody and across the open country north of Mozdok. Encountering stubborn resistance, they are fighting violent battles in all sectors. Particularly severe fighting is reported before Stepnoe, the northernmost point of the advance. Soviet tanks are prominent in the battle, and they have skilfully avoided a German ambush, by-passing and turning to annihilate it.

More details are available today of the condition of Hoth's trapped armies. Threatened by the death of their families should they surrender – for Hitler is believed to have issued such an order – some men are preferring suicide. In some units food is running low. Prisoners report that their diet included cats' and horses' entrails. Under cover of darkness deserters find their way to the Russian lines.

Tales of Stalingrad's defenders have become a legend but two new stories are published today. One is that of a cat, Mourka, which used to carry written reports on the enemy's gun emplacements from a group of Russian scouts to a house across the street where the company kitchen was established. The other is of a Red Army man who was killed when he was repairing a field telephone cable. When his corpse was found it was seen that the man had gripped two ends of the wire in his teeth. Contact was thus established and, as one writer states today, orders from headquarters passed through the hero's body.

90 January 1943

['There are always persons' observed a staff writer, inspired by the example of Mourka the cat, 'ready to expose the petty weaknesses of the great and to attribute to them motives lower than the heroic . . . The company kitchen was situated in the house to which Mourka bore dispatches, and some, with the cavilling peculiar to vulgar minds, will see in this more than a coincidence. That he was warmly greeted in the kitchen after his perilous journey we may rest assured. That he took an innocent pleasure in looking forward to the welcome of his comrades we may perhaps imagine. Beyond that the name of Mourka must never be coupled with a breath of doubt. He has shown himself worthy of Stalingrad, and whether for cat or man there can be no higher praise.']

POSE AS A REAR GUNNER

Ralph Eric Fraser, 54, a Home Guard, described as a labour manager, of Mildenhall Road, Clapton, E., was at Bow Street Police Court yesterday fined £50 and ordered to pay £25 costs by Mr McKenna for 'making a statement that he had acted as a rear gunner in a bomber over Germany, having reasonable cause to believe that it would be likely to interfere with the performance of police duties'. He pleaded 'Guilty'.

The charge had been reduced from the common law misdemeanour of causing a public mischief.

Mr H. A. K. Morgan, prosecuting, said that Fraser was employed as labour manager by Lonsdale, Hands Company, Limited, constructional engineers. When he arrived at work on 22 December he apparently looked tired, and said: 'I did not get home until 3 o'clock this morning. I was over Germany in a bomber last night as a rear gunner. I never felt so lonely in my life.'

That story, said counsel, was quite untrue. Fraser had spent the previous day with his family and did not leave the house. The story was the sort of one which might have been made by a silly, conceited young man seeking self glory, but it was an incredibly stupid one for a man of Fraser's age and respectability to make. He afterwards elaborated it to the firm's welfare officer, and at the request of the director, Mr Tanby, he gave a lecture to the staff on his adventures. Another director introduced him to a journalist, Mr Charles Graves, who told him he did not believe his story. Mr Graves communicated with the *Daily Express* and the *Daily Mail*, and Fraser gave them a convincing story which was published in both papers. Next day, at a staff lunch, the firm gave him a cheque for £25, but to his credit he did not cash the cheque, and he had made no money out of his story.

When the Air Ministry read the newspaper reports it was realized that the story, if true, was a most serious matter. The rear gunner of a bomber had the life of the crew in his hands, and anyone who allowed an inexperienced person in a bomber would have committed a most serious offence. Inquiries were at once made by officers of the Provost Marshal's department, Bomber Command, and Detective-inspector Freeman, and they were kept busy for hours.

Mr Claude Hornby, for the defence, said that Fraser had been more a fool than a knave.

12 January 1943

THE IDEAL CUP OF TEA

Standardized excellence in tea-making is the aim of a 16-page booklet, complete with diagrams and photographs, which has just been issued for the guidance of the staffs of Navy, Army, and Air Force Institutes.

As long ago as last summer experts reported that the tea in NAAFI canteens had improved immensely, an opinion that was confirmed by members of the services themselves. But it was felt that the matter was so important that a carefully prepared pamphlet was justified. This contains many interesting facts. For example, it is pointed out that if one gallon of tea were wasted each day, through overmaking, in every NAAFI canteen, there would be a total wastage in a year, not counting fuel, over the whole organization of more than 50,000,000 cups of tea, and that this is equivalent to £250,000 in cash.

There are lots of 'don'ts', as well as 'do's' in the instructions on tea-making, and emphasis is placed on the vital necessity of cleanliness and the proper handling of equipment for the production of the ideal cup of tea. The positive side of the question is urged in practical style.

'The tea leaf,' it is stated, 'only yields its best when it is subject to water at boiling point – i.e., bubbling fiercely. Boiling just means bubbling up – aeration – and freshly boiling water captures this aeration at its height and makes the best of tea. The length of time allowed for infusion is a very important factor in tea-making. Anything less than five minutes means that a large proportion of the goodness of the tea will be thrown away while the tea poured will be weak. Adding new tea to an old brew is just as bad as putting new wine into old bottles, particularly if the tea has already been milked.'

26 April 1943

'. . . instructions on tea-making'
[THE IDEAL CUP OF TEA]

OFFICIAL JARGON
A PAPER CONSUMPTION PUZZLE

A correspondent of *The Times* has written to inquire if the Ministry of Supply ever received the invitation which the Prime Minister issued, soon after he took office, to all heads of departments in the Civil Service to join in the effort to save everybody's time by condensing official papers and avoiding official jargon.

He explains that he has been driven to ask the question by the receipt this week of a 'Special Direction' made under the Control of Paper (No. 48) Order, 1942, which has come to him from the Deputy Controller of Paper for the Minister of Supply. The 'Special Direction' contains only two paragraphs, but as our correspondent says, 'What paragraphs!' They read as follows:

1. Notwithstanding anything contained in the Control of Paper (No. 48) Order, 1942, Directions Nos. 6 and 7, the Minister of Supply hereby directs in lieu of the provisions thereof that you shall not (subject to the provisions hereinafter contained) consume in the period 27 June 1943 to the 30 October 1943 in the production of the news-bulletins, magazines or periodicals mentioned in the first column of the schedule to the Special Direction (hereinafter referred to as the previous Direction) issued under the Control of Paper (No. 48) Order, 1942, under Control Reference 166/43, a quantity of paper (including any paper printed or made outside the United Kingdom) the aggregate weight of which exceeds the weight set out opposite that news-bulletin, magazine or periodical in the second column of that schedule plus one-seventeenth thereof.

2. The quantity of paper referred to in paragraph 1 hereof shall be increased or decreased as the case may be by the quantity of paper required for the production of one issue of any news-bulletin, magazine or periodical mentioned in the schedule to the said previous Direction, where the number of issues of that news-bulletin, magazine or periodical to be published in the period

covered by this present Direction is greater or less than the number of issues in one or each of the two preceding licence periods, if a corresponding reduction or increase as the case may be of consumption of paper has been effected in pursuance of any authorization given by the Minister in respect of either or each of those periods.

1 July 1943

A GERMAN SOLDIER'S RIDDLE

WITH THE EIGHTH ARMY Probing by Eighth Army patrols in the hill country seems to be reaching some sensitive German spots – not that the German rearguard resistance has become heavier on the ground, but the enemy's air activity has increased.

Our forward troops in small mountain villages have been subjected to short and sharp night raids in the last two nights, and at the same time the enemy has shown himself quick to resent our activity in the air, and to meet even a single reconnaissance aeroplane with extremely heavy anti-aircraft fire.

To some extent the *Luftwaffe*, long-range guns, and anti-aircraft guns are acting as a screen to the German rearguards, which the enemy seems to be withdrawing. It is hard to say where the German army will stand and fight, but it seems unlikely that it can be this side of the River Sangro. Comment on the German methods of withdrawal from an agreeably unlikely source is a riddle written out in a German soldier's note-book. 'What,' it runs, 'is the difference between Rommel and a watch? The watch always goes forward and says "*Ticktack*"; Rommel always goes backward and says "*Taktik*".'

28 October 1943

BATTLE OF THE KETTLE

Mr. H. W. Powell, ARP Controller of NAAFI, in an address at Caxton Hall yesterday in the London branch of the Institute of Civil Defence, told this story concerning the desire of a casualty service officer in the Midlands to buy an electric kettle for a first-aid post in a large public shelter.

'One of his officers saw a suitable kettle in a shop, but was told it could not be purchased without a permit. He asked the Ministry of Health for a permit to buy the kettle. They suggested that this was a matter for the Ministry of Supply to decide. The Ministry of Supply said that as shelters came under ARP, Home Security should decide whether he could buy the kettle or not.

'The Ministry of Home Security pushed him back to the Ministry of Health. My friend then kicked up a row, and finally a high official of the Ministry of Health telephoned saying that he was sorry not to be able to arrange for the purchase of the kettle, but that he had been to some trouble in the matter and through the kindness of the General Officer Commanding, Western Command, arrangements were being made for the supply of an Army mobile field kitchen.

'My friend replied that if such a contrivance were in fact delivered he would have it photographed going down the shelter steps and the photograph published in the Press. This threat secured him the kettle.'

Mr Powell told the story to support his contention that in some cases the Ministry of Home Security seemed to have no control over matters which were very much their concern. He referred to 'half-baked' directions issued by the Ministry, and said that these led to different readings 'according to the inclinations or even the lives of the local Pooh-Bahs'. He suggested a national civil defence service, with a proper control and recognition of all officers and staffs.

8 December 1943

UNDER THE OLD WITHY TREE

Treasure consisting of 81 sovereigns and 15 half-sovereigns dating from 1817 to 1857 was unearthed at Stanford-in-the-Vale, near Wantage, Berks, when a withy tree was being removed from a wall in the kitchen garden of the Old Mill House, the home of Lieutenant-Colonel and Mrs G. B. J. Kellie.

The operation necessitated demolition of part of the wall. When the wall fell an earthenware jar was smashed, disclosing the gold. At an inquest, held at the house on Saturday by Mr J. P. D. Ross Ormiston, of Wantage, Coroner for West Berks, the jury found that the coins had been intentionally hidden, and they ordered that 70 per cent of any proceeds received from the sale of the gold by the British Museum to the Bank of England should go to Henry Flippance, of Hatford, Faringdon, Colonel Kellie's gardener, who unearthed the jar, and 30 per cent to Colonel Kellie's five-year-old son, who ascertained the character of the find.

28 February 1944

SECRET AIRCRAFT DOWN IN SWEDEN

A Swedish military commission of investigation today went to Brosarp, in the south Swedish province of Scania, to examine a mysterious object which crashed there out of the sky yesterday. The first report from the Defence Staff announced that it was a remote-control aeroplane without a crew.

It lacked airscrew, tail, and under-carriage, and carried two globular mines or bombs, each 50 centimetres in diameter, which were hurled some 100 yards from the place of the crash without detonating. German lettering was found on parts that were retrieved.

Eye-witnesses described the object as a 'flying torpedo' with a long trail of fire and smoke: and they say it made a noise different from that of ordinary aeroplanes, which ceased before it made its final oblique dive to earth. It came from the direction of the German-occupied Danish island of Bornholm, in the Baltic, where the Germans are known to have been conducting 'secret weapon' experiments. Bornholm is roughly 40 miles from Brosarp.

13 May 1944

[Though the reference to the lack of a tail is puzzling, it is clear from later accounts that this was the first description of a V-1 flying bomb undergoing flight trials.]

NIGHTINGALE'S SONG IN THE DIN OF BATTLE

Nightingales are in the news. A correspondent with our forces in Italy has described how, on the Thursday night, while the greatest allied artillery offensive of the war crashed and echoed round the mountains, a nightingale sang continually. 'Above the deafening din came its sweet, shrill notes. It was singing before the barrage opened at 11 o'clock on Thursday night, and was still singing at 5 a.m. when the first bombers went over.'

It is not suggested, in this particular instance, that the nightingale sang because of the gunfire, indeed it is expressly stated that it was singing before the barrage opened, yet there is plenty of evidence, in this and in the last war, to suggest that nightingales do in fact redouble their efforts and sing their loudest amid the din of battle. It will not be forgotten how the heroic defenders of Calais were cheered by the song of the nightingales, and in this country, during the anxious period of Dunkirk, it seemed, to listeners in Sussex, Kent, and even here in Surrey, that never had the nightingales sung so gloriously as on those nights when the rumble of the guns in France came ever nearer and more threateningly to the English coast.

It has certainly seemed, in the last few weeks, that the nightingales have sung their best on the noisiest nights, and it would not be strange if this were so, for the literature of the last war is full of references to the nightingales heard by our men in France in intervals of comparative silence during the periods when the gunfire was most intense. It was so, too, in England during the Blitz, when one noticed, over and over again, how from the woods the nightingales replied to the distant crash of bombs, and the nearer the bombs the more vehement the song. Even now, in occasional nuisance raids, German aircraft arouse the nightingales to louder song.

16 May 1944

BEST ANSWER TO FLYING BOMBS

Judging by the results achieved to date, the best answer to Hitler's flying bomb is the latest British fighter, the Hawker Tempest. The main reasons for this machine's success are its very great speed and the high quality of its guns. Although the pilotless aircraft is faster at low altitudes than many known German fighters, the Tempest can overhaul it without difficulty; and one accurate burst of fire from its cannon is usually sufficient to blow the bomb to pieces in mid-air or to send it and its winged carrier crashing into the sea or on open ground.

During a stay of a night and day at a fighter airfield in southern England I have had a chance of seeing two Tempest squadrons – and ground defences – in action, and in that time both added to their score; and AA fire blew to pieces one robot that had sneaked overland a short distance while fighters were busy elsewhere.

One squadron belonging to a station commanded by Wing Commander R. P. Beamont, DSO, DFC and Bar, added to its score just as night was falling. Fighters were on patrol when, from the direction of the Channel, came a sound like that of an angry bee. A tiny speck of light appeared over the horizon, growing bigger every second, and the buzz and light soon synchronized themselves into what appeared to be a meteor with a flaming orange-red tail. Near the coast unseen guns opened fire from either flank and from directly underneath. Red and white tracer shot up in streams, coning the intruder, but it flew straight through it unharmed. Almost immediately the distinctive noise of a fighter's engine could be heard in hot pursuit of the fast receding 'meteor'. It had not gone far when more tracer shot across the sky, horizontally this time. There was a blinding flash, and flaming pieces of wreckage showered to the ground. The next was a victory for the gun.

Then the fighter station went to bed, by the sound of night fighters from other stations and of periodic bursts of gunfire and of ceaseless vigil. Before it was light every one on the airfield was roused by the roar of engines of Tempests being warmed up in readiness for another busy day. Dawn was only just breaking when Flight Lieutenant A. R. Moore, of Reading, destroyed his fifth flying bomb in a week to make him the squadron's top scorer. This one did not even reach land; it was shot into the Channel some distance out, sending up a fountain of water which could be seen for miles.

Attacks All the Way Over

Our ground and air defences have been so organized that the flying bombs can be attacked at all stages of their journey, even off the French coast when they are still climbing and have not, therefore, attained their maximum speed, which is well over 300 m.p.h. Our fighters so time their attacks as to ensure that they bring down their target on open ground. Some inevitably escape destruction, but the measure of success against them is shown by the fact that the Tempests on this station have destroyed a high percentage of the total number sighted from the air.

One of the pilots described what it is like to attack one of these flying projectiles. 'As you close up on it,' he said, 'it looks like a large flame with wings sticking out on either side. Because it is so small it is not easy to hit, but the flying bomb is very vulnerable. If your bullets strike home on the jet unit, the whole thing catches fire and it goes down with a crash: if you hit the bomb, the robot blows up. When we started attacking these things we trod warily, shooting from long range, but as we have got experience of this new form of attack we find that we can close in sometimes to 100 yards. If you are close when the bomb goes up you sometimes fly through the debris, and some of our Tempests have come back with their paint scorched: some have been turned over on their backs by the force of the explosion but the pilot feels no effect except an upward jolt.

'Often it is not necessary to hit your target badly. A few bullets sometimes upset the gyro (automatic pilot) and then the robot does some queer manoeuvres and crashes straight in. We can catch them without undue difficulty, and making these attacks is helping to make our shooting very accurate. It is easy to knock them down and we are confident of getting a very high proportion. During one period we saw seven, and got them all.'

The first fighter pilot to shoot down what the RAF men call a 'doodlebug' was Flight Sergeant Maurice Rose, of Glasgow, and he rejoined his unit only just in time to earn the distinction. Three days before he had had to make a forced landing behind the allied lines in Normandy while out on an offensive patrol. He recrossed the Channel in a supply vessel and soon afterwards went up to try out his new machine. A flying bomb came buzzing across the Channel and he promptly blew it up in mid-air. It was all over almost as quickly as that.

22 June 1944

[A few days before, *The Times* had relayed fanciful German accounts of the new 'dynamite meteor' secret weapon. The whole of the South of England, stated the German press, was shaken as though by an earthquake. London and the south coast were hidden by a dense pall of smoke, so that exact observation by German reconnaissance planes of the holocaust was impossible.]

HOW TO AVOID BLAST FROM BOMBS: HOME OFFICE ADVICE

Wherever You May Be Do not be afraid to be the first to take precautions when you hear a bomb coming.

17 July 1944

AN AWKWARD EXCHANGE

The performance of *Fig Leaves and Apple Sauce*, a *revue* due to be presented at the Palace Theatre, Bath, last night, had to be postponed until today. A railway truck containing the scenery, properties, and costumes went astray, and in its place one containing the instruments of a complete orchestra arrived at Bath.

22 August 1944

HAIRCUTS UNDER FIRE

NEAR MEUSE-ESCAUT CANAL Coming northward this morning from the stricken Hechtel crossroads, the scene of days of fierce fighting which ended yesterday, I have before me a quaint sidelight on this extraordinary war.

Here we are perhaps two miles from the bridge seized intact by our armour, and a fair amount of shelling is going on, both ways. There is an estaminet being used as an infantry company's headquarters, and some of the men have a bivouac in the garden, which is all open to the road. They have brought a chair from the house and have formed a queue for hair-cutting in the warm sunshine.

There is nothing very remarkable about this except that

the hairdresser is a German prisoner, a cheerful creature in the blue uniform of a *Luftwaffe* ground battalion in which he was the regimental barber before our men captured him complete with his excellent kit of hairdressing tools. They are not going to let him go down to the cage till he has 'done his stuff' for all who need him.

Shells from our medium guns are whistling over constantly, and now and then something from the enemy that seems heavy arrives in our neighbourhood. That is the signal for the barber and his clients to part company for a time, some to jump into slit trenches, and those near enough to the house to step quickly inside.

18 September 1944

HITLER'S TEMPERS

In an enemy document dated 9 August which has come into Eighth Army hands a political education officer of the German 1st Parachute Division states: 'Officers must counteract by all possible means, and with conviction, the assertions made by the enemy, as well as even some of our own people, that the Führer goes mad with rage and when he is in that state tears down curtains, bites the carpet in his rage, and rolls in convulsions on the floor.'

The document adds that there are witnesses who know that Hitler is 'well above such lack of control, though many a man in the street, if he were exposed to the disappointments and grief which the Führer has to bear, would have gone under long ago.'

20 September 1944

NO PLACE FOR A DOG

All the way from Euston to Holyhead on the packed Irish mail many passengers had to stand. But in one compart-

'. . . such lack of control'
[HITLER'S TEMPERS]

ment, it was stated by an LMS official at Crewe yesterday, a large Dalmatian dog occupied a seat for the whole 260 miles. When its owner, Mrs G. Richard, of Goodge Place, London, W., was asked by officials and passengers to remove it, she refused, even for a first class passenger seeking a third class seat. Mrs Richards was fined the maximum of £2, with £7 17s costs, for allowing the dog to remain in a passenger coach. Mr H. W. G. Garnett, for the LMS, said Mrs Richards told the guard that the dog was nervous. To a police officer, he added, she said she hoped a bomb would drop on him for reporting her.

11 October 1944

A PICKPOCKET'S MISTAKE

In Tottenham Court Road on Saturday a pickpocket approached a well-dressed man, furtively placed an experienced hand into a bulging pocket, and removed the contents. Suddenly a yell was heard above the noise of the traffic and the pickpocket ran down a side street. He had picked from the pocket of a magician a small non-poisonous snake, which wriggled down a drain and disappeared.

11 November 1946

GROUNDNUT STAFF FINDS WATER

DAR-ES-SALAAM Millions of gallons of never-failing water now soaking away uselessly into the sand will be dammed, distributed, and used both for the groundnut scheme and by the local natives as the result of a water crisis at Nachingwea (Southern Province).

The difficulty of borehole drilling in the hard deep rock caused the engineers of the ground-nut scheme to draw unduly heavily on the local village well, which showed signs of drying up. The consumption of water had to be drastically reduced and efforts to find water quickly were extended to a wider field. Informed by a local African of the existence of some springs 16 miles away, the engineers found that these could be enlarged into a 5-million gallon dam with a steady inflow of 8,000 gallons an hour, and all within pipable distance.

But local Africans were reluctant to start work on the pool. It was the special preserve of a local witch doctor, who was a Mganga (practitioner in beneficent magic) as distinct from a Mchawi (specialist in black magic). The pool had been 'his' since a drowned man's body was recovered as a result – so Mr Strachey was told on the spot last Thursday – of the Mganga's efforts.

Advised by a member of their staff with long local

experience, the groundnut cultivators got over the difficulty by recognizing the 'rights' of the Mganga and obtaining his approval of their work in enlarging his pool and making the water useful. He also pronounced a spell 'guaranteeing' the safety of the new dam. His fee was one shilling.

8 June 1948

[Despite this promising start, the Groundnut Scheme, darling of Mr John Strachey, Minister for Food, later came to be seen as the worst agricultural failure of recent years.]

THE KING'S MESSAGE 'SPLICE THE MAINBRACE'

The King has sent the following message to Admiral Sir Patrick Brind, Commander-in-Chief, Far East Station:

'Please convey to the commanding officer and ship's company of HMS *Amethyst* my hearty congratulations on their daring exploit to rejoin the Fleet. The courage, skill, and determination shown by all on board have my highest commendation. Splice the mainbrace. – George R.'

1 August 1949

[Three days later the People's Dispensary for Sick Animals announced, subject to the recommendation of the ship's company, that Simon, the cat on HMS *Amethyst*, was to be awarded the Dickin medal for valour. He was the first cat to receive this honour. Despite injuries sustained during the shelling he had played a vital role by keeping down rats and thus preserving dwindling stocks of food.]

PAXTON'S DREAM: 11-MILE BOULEVARD WITH A GLASS ROOF

Miss Violet Markham, granddaughter of Joseph Paxton, the designer of the Crystal Palace, yesterday described to the Royal Society of Arts a vast boulevard which her grandfather planned to encircle London.

He drew up the scheme three years after the 1851 Exhibition. The plans were submitted to a committee of the House of Commons which was studying the problem of communications caused by the congestion of London traffic. The committee, though staggered by the grandiose scheme, was much attracted by some aspects and approved some principles of the plan, but the House of Commons would have none of the idea.

Paxton's Great Victorian Way was to be iron roofed with glass, 11½ miles long, 72 ft broad, and 100 ft high. Houses and shops were to be built under cover of the arcade with an ordinary roadway between them. Eight lines of railways were to run on a raised corridor 20 ft high. The scheme was to cost £34m., but Paxton was convinced that rentals would pay the interest on the capital. The boulevard was to start at the Royal Exchange, cross the Thames at Rotherhithe by a special bridge, pass through Lambeth, cross the river again at Westminster, and go through Victoria, Belgravia, Kensington and Notting Hill to Paddington, whence it would return to the Royal Exchange through Islington.

Miss Markham said that few people today had ever heard of the scheme and even the elaborate and beautiful plans exhibited in the House of Lords had disappeared.

16 November 1950

ICICLE DEATH IN 1776 COMMEMORATED

A tablet was placed yesterday at the parish church of St Michael and All Angels, Bampton, Devon, to commemorate the death in 1776 of the son of the parish clerk who was killed outside the church tower when struck in the eye by a falling piece of ice. His name is unknown, but his fate is recorded in the church records. The inscription on the tablet reads:

Bless my eyes,
Here he lies,
In a sad pickle,
Killed by an icicle.

The tablet, given to the church by a parishioner, has been placed in the tower above a stone originally laid to commemorate the tragedy. This stone contained the same verse but the words have become obliterated.

10 February 1951

CHEAPER ATOMIC ENERGY – PRESIDENT PERON'S CLAIM

BUENOS AIRES General Peron announced at a Press conference yesterday that Argentina has discovered how to harness atomic energy cheaply without using uranium. He said that thermo-nuclear reactions were obtained in experiments on 16 February at a pilot plant on Huemul Island, in Lake Nahuel Huapi, near San Carlos de Bardoche, northern Patagonia.

The experiments were carried out by a group of scientists working under Professor Richter, aged 42, an Austrian-born scientist who is now a naturalized Argentine citizen.

. . . A number of electronic robots designed and built in Argentina, each doing the work of 500 men, are in operation at the Huemel Island atomic plant, according to Professor Richter. He said the plant had neither cyclotrons nor Van de Graaff machines, as they were not needed in his system. Only a reduced number of technicians were actually working on the project since the bulk of the work was done by robots.

26 March 1951

[The Australian nuclear physicist Professor (later Sir) Mark Oliphant remarked that there was nothing impossible about this claim. 'It is extremely interesting if true,' he said.]

A COELACANTH IDENTIFIED

DURBAN The specimen of a prehistoric Coelacanth found near Madagascar – the species of fish that lived over 50 million years ago which may throw light on the theory of man's evolution from sea creatures – reached Durban tonight in a heavily guarded box. It was brought from an island in the Mozambique Channel by Professor J. L. B. Smith, of Rhodes University, in the military aircraft specially ordered by Dr Malan, the Prime Minister.

The fish is to be named *Malania anjouanae*, after Dr Malan, and will be flown early tomorrow to Grahamstown. It has been preserved with formalin.

The fish was caught with hook and line by an Arab, Ahmed Hussein, and was nearly sold in the fish market.

Professor Smith describes this as 'one of the greatest scientific discoveries of all time'. He said the 'fish with arms' was caught by an island fisherman in about 65 ft of water off the island of Anjouan, in the Comoro group, 200 miles west of Madagascar. It weighs 100 lb.

The coelacanth had been kept in formalin for 10 days while Mr Eric Hunt, who lives on the island, cabled Professor Smith. Describing how he first saw the fish, the professor said it was not perfect, but its condition was more than satisfactory. The islanders told him that two or three similar fish were caught each year in the same region.

30 December 1952

£100,000 FRAUD

A Paris court today sentenced two men to four years' imprisonment and a third to 18 months for defrauding Baron Scipone de Roure of 100 million francs (about £100,000).

The three men, posing as senior officers and members of France's counter-espionage organization, persuaded Baron Scipone de Roure to buy a flask of 'uranium' which proved to be sand. They also persuaded him to part with considerable sums, and his wife's diamond necklace, over a two-year period, in the belief that the money was being spent in the interests of French national defence.

The magistrate said that the affair was like 'something out of an American film or a circus'. It was stated that the Baron had an asbestos vest specially made to protect him from 'radiation', and took the flask of 'uranium' everywhere with him, even when he went fishing.

6 June 1953

'ABOMINABLE SNOW BABY'

DELHI Mrs Monica Jackson, leader of the British women's expedition to the Himalayas, said they found tracks in the snow which their Sherpa guide said were made by 'abominable snowmen'. On the previous day they had found another set of tracks which their Sherpa said belonged to an 'abominable snow-baby'. They were only about four inches long. 'Our Sherpa insisted that they were those of a *yeti* and when we said that was impossible as they were too small, he said, "Yes, yes, this is an eight-year-old *yeti*." '

10 June 1955

TENOR SWALLOWS FALSE MOUSTACHE

The Belgian tenor, M. Jan Verbeek, inadvertently swallowed his false moustache during Act II of Boito's opera, *Mefistofele*, at the Casino Theatre, Vichy, today. M. Verbeek was able to continue singing, but had visible difficulty with his high notes, which he afterwards attributed to the violent irritation set up by hairs sticking to the back of his throat. A similar accident, it may be recalled, befell Mr Walter Midgley in a performance of *Rigoletto* at Covent Garden two years ago.

15 July 1955

THIEF TRAPPED BY HIS SCHOOL ESSAY

BONN The case of Aschaffenburg's missing rabbits, which had baffled some of Bavaria's best-known detectives, has been solved.

The rabbits were stolen from an elementary school teacher in a village near Aschaffenburg. The theft was reported to the police but when they admitted failure he decided to make an investigation himself, and gave his pupils the task of writing an essay on 'our favourite Sunday meal'.

He was not disappointed: two of the boys described, with obvious enjoyment, the roasted rabbits they had eaten on the previous Sunday. This was their undoing. The police were informed, a confession was obtained, and an arrest was made. It seems that considerable importance is attached to the security of Aschaffenburg's rabbits, for the culprit has been sentenced to one year's imprisonment.

10 May 1956

CHILDREN BRING IN WORMS GALORE

CANBERRA The Department of Microbiology at the

'. . . violent irritation'
[TENOR SWALLOWS FALSE MOUSTACHE]

Australian National University recently advertised for earthworms at 20s a lb. It needed the worms in connexion with an experiment designed to increase understanding of muscle chemistry in mammals. A compound found in worms is apparently related to the contraction of muscles.

The department expected 10 lb. It reckoned without the industry and enterprise of Canberra's children, who turned up yesterday in hundreds, carrying tins from which they produced more than 1 cwt of worms. The laboratory staff worked until 2 a.m. today extracting the compound.

When more children arrived today the department had already stored in its freezer all the worms it wanted, so the market closed.

10 September 1958

SPEECHES DISTURBED BY KNITTING

A resolution saying that knitting should be banned at all conferences was passed by the eastern area British Legion women's sections at their London conference yesterday. 'It is felt,' said the resolution, 'that delegates cannot concentrate on their notes.'

Mrs W. J. Roberts, of Wymondham, Norfolk, who proposed, said that the clicking of knitting needles drew attention from speeches. 'We have even had knitting on the platform. A conference is not the place for knitting.'

12 February 1959

TIDDLYWINK CROWN – BOMBER COMMAND TEAM'S CHALLENGE

A new challenger for the British tiddlywink crown entered the lists over the weekend when a team from RAF Bomber Command headquarters surprised even its own supporters by defeating the London School of Economics by 72 points to 49.

As yet unrecognized by both the Royal Air Force and the English Tiddlywinks Association, this embryo team hopes to show what it can do before applying for official recognition. Spurred on by the words of the Rev. E. A. Willis, general secretary of the English Association, that 'the world is now looking to tiddlywinks in its need to get back to the primeval simplicity of life', the Bomber Command team has adopted as its motto 'squidge hard, squidge sure'.

The team is aiming high in its battle for recognition, and after taking on Oxford and Cambridge hopes to do battle with the tiddlers in the Houses of Parliament.

17 March 1959

DOG'S RIGHT TO GO TO CHURCH: RECTOR DEFIES CRITICS

The Rector of Chedzoy, a village near Bridgwater, the Rev. Mervyn Basil Bazell, has a 14-year-old Kerry Blue terrier, Pet, which accompanies him to church on weekdays for matins and evensong and on Sunday afternoons to the children's service.

Some of the villagers are objecting to this, and one of them, Mr Roy House, a member of the parochial church council, said his children had been disturbed at their prayers on Sunday afternoons by the dog moving along pews and tickling their legs. He said that at the last meeting of the parochial church council he proposed that the dog should be barred from the church, but the rector refused to put the resolution to the meeting.

Mr House added that he and other members of the church council had consulted the Rural Dean, Prebendary E. H. Hughes Davies, and he had stated that he thought there was nothing that could be done to stop it. Mr House said that if the dog was not kept out of the church they would take the matter up with the Archdeacon of Taunton, the Rev. G. F. Hilder.

Another resident, Mrs G. Baker, said that at a christening which she attended the dog came sniffing round the front.

No Objection Before

The rector says he has held a living since 1933 and his dog has always accompanied him to church. Before he went to Chedzoy in November he had a parish in Staffordshire, and no one had objected before. He said: 'I regard all animals as God's creatures, and I would never turn any animal out of church. If other people wish to bring their dogs into my church they will be welcomed so long as the dogs are well behaved and under control.'

Referring to an objection that the dog carried dirt into the church, the rector said: 'The amount is negligible. I take far greater concern at the spiritual mud which is brought into church by certain people through their venom, malice and uncharitableness.'

18 March 1959

[On 31 March a notice on the West Door of Southwell Minster, Nottingham, announced 'Dogs Welcome'. 'During the warm weather,' explained the Provost, 'this would save dogs suffering in the heat of locked cars while their owners enjoyed the cool interior of the Minster.']

UNOFFICIAL RABBITS OF HYDE PARK

It is no secret (though oddly few people seem aware of the fact) that for the seasonal sight of young rabbits gambolling among the daffodils one need at the moment stray no farther in central London than Hyde Park. Here, in a large enclosure near Knightsbridge known to *cognoscenti* as The Dell, a colony has been entrenched as long as anybody can remember – black ones, white ones, rabbit-coloured ones, and a very contended lot they look.

Understandably so. What with the unnatural enemy of myxomatosis and now the Government subsidizing rabbit clearance societies on a pound for pound basis, any rabbit could do worse than take cover in this metropolitan sanctuary.

Unsolved Mystery

The mystery is how the rabbits got there in the first place. One had always assumed these rodents were Civil servants, a modest item tucked away somewhere in the Ministry of Works estimates and a happy contrast to the dim view which the Ancient Monuments branch have never disguised they take of warrens in old ruins.

But inquiry revealed that this is not so. At least the Ministry declared through their spokesman that they did not even officially recognize the existence of these rabbits, though he admitted their attitude could perhaps fairly be called 'ambiguous'. For one thing, he admitted the Ministry have taken the trouble to put up a wire fence around them; for another that they do definitely make an attempt 'periodically' to reduce their numbers, without saying what happens to the evicted.

He emphasized, however, that actually the fence was not so much to keep the rabbits in as to keep them out of the rest of the park, including the plants in the rock garden.

Pests or Pets?

So where did the rabbits come from? Ministerial researches could not establish whether they began as pets or pests, i.e. which came first, the rabbits or the Park. They took it for granted that someone had once upon a time put one or two discarded pets there, but their official agreed it was possible that the first settlers had been wild rabbits indigenous to the terrain in its more rural days.

Possibly, therefore, apart from casual offerings, there is a secret society somewhere in London dedicated to their needs and dropping a sackful of new recruits over the fence whenever the fancy takes them.

What is abundantly obvious is that at present, whatever

their status, they are by no means dwindling. Ministerial conjecture puts the population at three or four families, normally about 16 rabbits, and untouched by myxomatosis. This week it was possible to count nearly a dozen on the surface, contemptuous of public gaze; how many more were busily breeding underground can only be imagined.

One big black rabbit lolloped up to a broken down fence which looked as if it might once have been intended to keep him out of one rock garden and hopped over it with Olympic aplomb.

It seems to be agreed, anyway, that the rabbits do add a touch of bucolic pleasantness to Hyde Park, though as always there are exceptions; one citizen, not noticeably misanthropic, grumbled with some heat about the mess made by those 'darned rabbits'. Conceivably, the day may even come, if the rabbit clearance societies have their way, when this will become one of the last outposts of British rabbit society and even countrymen will have to come up to London to see them.

7 April 1959

MAKING THE CRIME FIT THE PUNISHMENT

A man who was fined 20,000 francs (about £14) in Paris for breaking the glass of a street police box and setting off the alarm without a legitimate cause, explained to the magistrate that he happened to be standing near when someone came up, broke the glass, set the alarm going and then made off. When the police arrived they mistook him for the culprit, refused to accept his denials, and took him to the police station.

He was so annoyed at being unjustly accused that as soon as he was released he made for the nearest police signal, and heaved a stone at the glass. When a policeman arrived, he at once admitted his guilt, but this time the policeman refused to accept this admission. Eventually he convinced him that he was responsible and was charged.

15 July 1959

'BISHOP RIGHT TO GIVE AN OPINION'

Dr Sonald Soper, the Methodist leader, spoke about *Lady Chatterley's Lover* to a crowd of 300 people at Speakers' Corner, Marble Arch, yesterday.

'We are a curious people,' he said. 'A book such as this is no sooner adjudged to be non-pornographic than there is a rush to the other extreme – to regard it as the fifth gospel. I am delighted that the book has been reprieved. It is an excellent piece of literature and it is a sincere attempt by the author to present one side of married life.

'What I object to is that the book will take on that holy communion look. This is sheer balderdash.

'As for the Bishop of Woolwich, well, he has been hauled over the coals but nevertheless I think he was right to express an opinion. I only wish a few more bishops would step into the limelight instead of hiding their thoughts.'

7 November 1960

[The Bishop of Woolwich, the Right Rev. John Robinson, had indeed been 'hauled over the coals' by the Archbishop for taking part in the Penguin Books trial, as a witness for the defence. In the Archbishop's judgement the Bishop was mistaken in thinking that he could take part 'without becoming a stumbling block and a cause of offence to many ordinary Christians'.

After the jury had found in favour of Penguin Books, Sir Allen Lane commented on the heavy costs of the case: 'We should not get very drunk on the change from £10,000.' Penguin was intending to increase their printing from 200,000 to 500,000 as a result of the verdict.]

HELLO AND FAREWELL

The voice of the hullo-girl will before long be heard no more. The telephones are being mechanized and we shall soon be at the mercy of the Dial. Instead of 'Sorry, there's no reply' or 'Line out of order' there will be an irritating burr like the hoarse humming of sickly bumble bees.

I write of the little country exchanges, particularly of my own in the village over the river. Like many of my neighbours I view the future with fear and loathing. We are not anxious about the young ladies themselves. They are not being forced to resign. No more will be recruited and, the Postmaster General assured Parliament, matrimony will absorb those who now manipulate our lines of communication. I am not in the least surprised. What can a young man want more than tact, intelligence, good humour, patience and courtesy, combined with good looks?

Neighbourly Tradition

Our exchange is run by a couple of our local girls, who know all about the majority of their customers. The girls' identities change over the years as they leave to make some country lad happy: but the tradition remains, the grand old tradition of neighbourliness. You may not know your operator personally; but she knows you.

I give the number of my friend Garth Christian. 'Sorry, Mr Christian's gone to the library at Lewes and won't be back till after tea' our admirable operator tells me and saves me threepence.

Sometimes I have to speak to a fruit farmer who lives next door to the exchange. I lift my receiver; give his number. 'He's out picking strawberries. He'll be there for another hour at least, I reckon. I'll ring you when he comes in.' How often has the kindly guardian at the switchboard told me that or something similar: and never failed to keep her promise to ring me.

A neighbour, whose forebears were at home when the Conqueror came, insists that this spontaneous friendliness is peculiar to Sussex, where we hold the official and bureaucratic attitude in contempt: but foreigners as far away as Somerset and Yorkshire have spoken to me with enthusiasm of the helpful girls at their country exchanges.

Yet I doubt whether in any county but Sussex the young lady at the exchange would have got the vet for me on the Sunday when my goat Charybdis got into terrible trouble when about to kid. Her baby had died before it was born.

The Sick Goat

During the war I had two goats of the rare old English breed: none of your hornless docile Saanens or Toggenburgs or Nubians but the genuine home product, vigorous, black and white, with graceful sloping horns, independent, as clever as monkeys. We called them Scylla and Charybdis because it was dangerous to get between them.

Charybdis was in a desperate state. The vet lives 15 miles away. I hastened to call him up, and was immediately face to face with disaster. His telephone was out of order. 'That's bad,' I exclaimed. 'Is there anything serious?' asked my exchange.

'There is,' said I. 'One of my goats looks as if she'll die if something isn't done at once. And I doubt if I can do it myself. I must have the vet.'

'Oh! We can't have that,' said the sympathetic young lady: 'Hold on. I'll try to get him for you. What's his name and address?' I told her, and listened as she set about solving the problem.

First she got on to her colleague at the vet's exchange and explained the position: a dying goat, a vet with a telephone out of order. She gave the vet's name and address. 'Could you ring the nearest subscriber to him?' she suggested.

It was a masterly manoeuvre. The charming girl at the other end traced the vet's nearest neighbour and rang. As soon as I heard the neighbour reply my heart fell. It was a female dragon's voice, cold, precise, emphatic.

'. . . Scylla and Charybdis'
[HELLO AND FAREWELL]

A Dragon Tamed

My vet's exchange, her duty done, retired. My friend took over. Softly she began: 'There's a gentleman who has a goat very ill –'

'*What* did you say?' the dragon demanded.

'A goat,' the undaunted girl replied: 'And we have to have a vet or she will die. And his line's out of order. You're his nearest neighbour.'

'This has *nothing* to do with *me*,' the dragon said haughtily.

'Of course not,' my grand little ally pursued (to this day I do not know who she was), 'but I'm sure you would never refuse to help a suffering animal.'

'Well, what do you want me to *do*?' asked the voice, without enthusiasm, true, but showing some willingness to help. I nearly thanked her: but affairs were in capable hands. 'We wondered,' cooed my friend in need, 'if you could please inform the vet that a goat is very ill at –' she gave my name and address.

'I shall send my chauffeur with the message as soon as he returns,' the dragon said with great dignity, adding: 'It's only because I belong to Our Dumb Friends League that I do so.'

'Oh, thank you,' said my excellent ambassadress, wisely deciding to leave it at that. When the dragon had cut off she observed: 'What an old battle-axe.'

'Never mind,' said I, 'you were splendid.' She asked me to let her know what happened. I did so later. All was well. The vet arrived in time and Charybdis was saved.

Would a Dial . . . ?

Would a Dial have been able to do anything remotely resembling this act of charity, ingenuity, and courage?

Would a Dial, when I used the telephone for the first time when I came home after a serious operation in the spring, have cried: 'Oh, how nice to hear your voice! Are you quite all right again? We were quite worried about you, having to be taken away in an ambulance early in the morning and all that.'

I was told that when they heard I was in hospital the telephone girls, every time anyone used the instrument from my home, made a point of asking how I was. My goat girl had gone seven years before: but the same humanity and neighbourly concern are there.

This is in the green heart of Sussex. What happens in great cities I do not know. Only once have I had any unofficial conversation with a metropolitan damsel. I have ears like an old jack rabbit. I can hear the hoot of the tawny owl in the teeth of a south-westerly gale, and the weird love screech of the badger in the distant wood across the river. But I failed to catch an observation made to me by a London operator whose refined accent puzzled me for a moment and I asked her to repeat it. 'You ought to get a deaf-aid,' she snapped. We had Words. I don't care if they mechanize her.

11 January 1961

RUSSIA'S GOATS IN THE CUPBOARD

by **Monitor**

Just so that they would feel more at home, the first thing that the Kolovorotov family did when they moved from their dilapidated suburban house to a new sixth-floor flat in Moscow was to release a boxful of cockroaches. Petya, aged 10, began building a dovecote on the balcony, while grandmother washed Mashka, the goat, in the bath before installing her in the wardrobe.

'Why are some individuals newly installed in comfortable, modern and sparkling clean flats seized with a mania for turning them into half-ruined lairs?' Why do some people throw themselves at their new housing 'like troglodytes at a cornered mammoth'? Taking up a theme which has concerned Soviet newspapers like *Vechernaya Moskva* and *Sovyetskaya Rossiya* for some time, the current issue of the satirical weekly *Krokodil* urges harsher penalties for specialists in shooting down electric light bulbs, 'masters in the art of mural decoration', and generally those responsible for making many a new apartment house look as if it had withstood a siege.

11 April 1961

OSLO LIBRARY BAN ON DONALD DUCK

Donald Duck is one of the most popular cartoon figures in Norway, but he has been banned from Oslo's municipal libraries. The ban is temporary, and Donald himself is the innocent victim of the ceaseless linguistic dispute which is a widespread pastime in Norway.

Norway is a bilingual country. The majority speak the so-called *riksmal* which, however, is being stripped of its linguistic purity by constant efforts to merge it with the so-called *landsmal*. This is based on peasant dialects and is spoken nowhere in the country except in the state radio broadcasts.

Nevertheless, *landsmal* has its determined adherents who are now protesting against what they consider the ridiculing of *landsmal* in the Donald Duck series. The cartoons which brought Donald into disgrace concerned a strange country where people were said to be square and the hens were believed to produce square eggs. But these square people incidentally spoke *landsmal*. This was too serious to be taken as a joke by the *landsmal* crusaders.

Now a library committee is investigating whether square people do speak *landsmal* in real life, or whether this presentation of Donald Duck's adventures is tantamount to a libellous treatment of *landsmal* in view of its position as one of the official languages in Norway.

Less serious people get a good laugh while this deliberation goes on. Donald himself is reported to be more popular than before, especially among grown-ups.

25 April 1963

BANK NOTES 'WHITER THAN WHITE'

Five-pound notes may be blue, one-pound notes green, and 10s notes brown, but after they have been in a washing machine with a detergent they all come out whiter than white.

This interesting sidelight on the affluent society is contained in *The Bank of England Quarterly Bulletin*, published today. In an article on mutilated notes, it states: 'It is evident that some detergents could claim among their other characteristics the ability to reduce a bank note to a perfectly white sheet.'

Washing machines, according to the article, are now probably the most common source of damage. Other causes include 'the appetites of dogs and other pets and even of small children', fire and water, and imprudent methods of storing notes.

The growing use of banking facilities had cut down the last cause, it is stated, but the remains of rotted notes which had been buried in the garden or hidden under floor boards were still presented from time to time. 'The temptation to foil the burglar by hiding a precious hoard of notes in the stove or up the chimney during the summer leads to many disasters when fires are lit later.'

Offered for Payment

Last year 193,000 badly mutilated notes were presented to the bank for payment, representing 158 notes for each million in circulation. Slightly damaged notes, it is explained, could be exchanged by members of the public at banks and post offices, but to qualify for payment this way a note must consist of more than half the original area, contain the 'promise to pay', at least one-third of the signature, and more than one complete number.

The number of notes paid for each year was about five million. Notes more badly damaged must be sent to the Bank of England.

Is the Bank of England planning to make its notes more detergent proof and less liable generally to mutilation? At the Bank yesterday the question was treated with a metaphorical raising of eyebrows. 'Nothing is going to stop a small boy chewing up banknotes, or a detergent washing out the ink,' an official said. 'If we made bank notes of steel, somebody would probably put them on the railway line.'

11 September 1963

SAUSAGE TREE MYSTERY

The mystery of the Uganda sausage tree, which grows 12 lb fruits in a month at the end of a long stalk, something that should be impossible, was unfolded to the botany section by Dr M. J. P. Canny, Lecturer in Botany at Cambridge University, who has recently returned from Africa where he studied the habits of this odd tree.

How so much organic material moved so fast through so narrow a stalk was a problem shown strikingly by the sausage fruits. The transfer of sugar into the fruits followed the same rules of diffusion as were obeyed by sugar diffusing in solution – but speeded up about 50,000 times, a physiological behaviour unique in living systems.

A layer of sugar in the bottom of a cup slowly spread into the liquid above by random motions of the molecules. In an unstirred cup of coffee, for the diffusion mixing to proceed until the top layer differed from the bottom by 1 per cent would take 1,000 years. The rate of transport of sugar in the sausage tree reached four grams an hour per square centimetre of the special tissues of the inner bark.

3 September 1964

TYING A KNOT IN THE ASTRONAUT'S HANDKERCHIEF

Memory improvement is big business in the United States, where nearly every magazine carries advertisements for

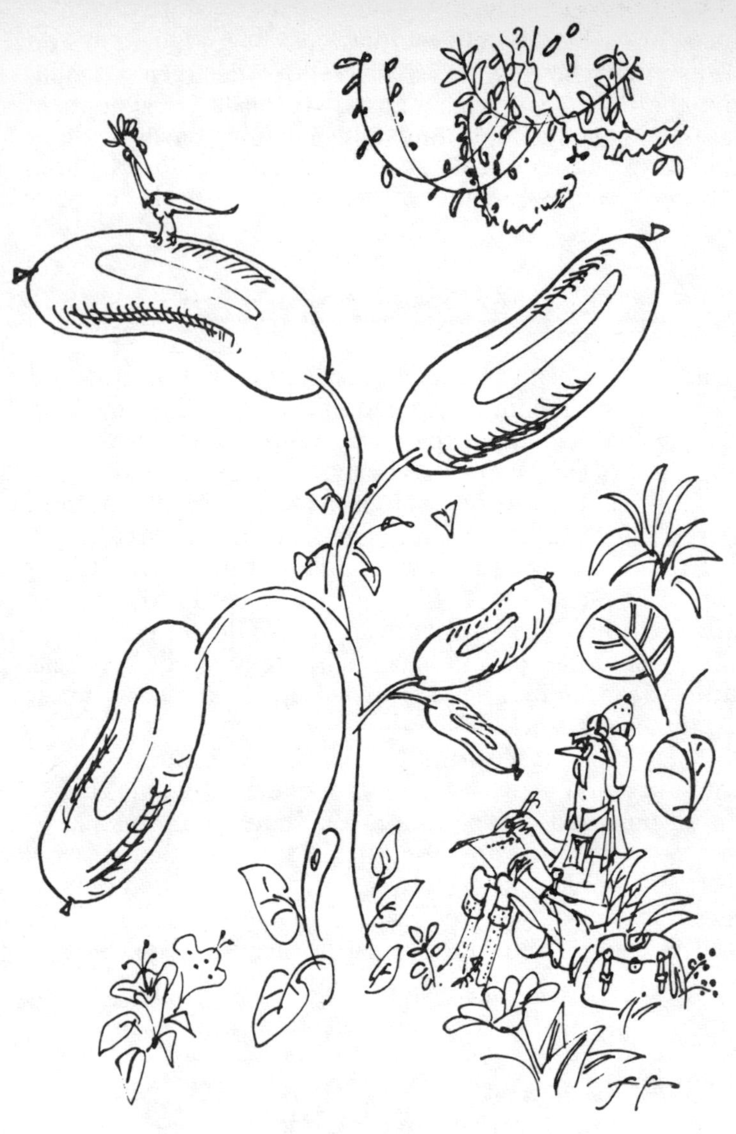

'. . . something that should be impossible'
[SAUSAGE TREE MYSTERY]

mental drills or ingenious props of one kind or another.

Now it has attracted the funds of a Government agency with the most formidable mnemonic problem of all in this complicated society. The manned spacecraft centre in Houston, Texas, has commissioned Honeywell, Inc., to test devices to log an astronaut's memory of the 101 things he may have to do properly to bring his vehicle safely home.

The centre observed that volumes of material on forgetfulness have mostly touched on verbal retention rather than visual or perceptual reactions. An astronaut must perform many complicated sequences of control correctly and in the right order, and there is a possibility that repeated rehearsals will not be effective in maintaining a specific skill such as reentry, especially after a long flight.

Star Points

Honeywell, which has a long experience of putting fallible humanity in orderly surroundings, are to spend five months and $49,990 (£17,850) on testing mechanical aids to memory more refined than a knotted handkerchief. One suggestion by the spacecraft centre is a six-pointed star, with each point tipped in a different colour – 12 o'clock yellow, 2 red, 4 blue, 6 green, 8 purple, and 10 orange. To each point would be attached an even-numbered month, from red February to yellow December, and an adjective chosen at random. For December the choice would be 'aloof'.

Groups of people would be given the star to study once a week for a given time, and then tested on their recollection six weeks later.

A more complicated star, with 12 points and colour reference involving sequences (red to mean one, three and five, for example, with a combination of otherwise unrelated adjectives), has also been suggested.

A judicious combination of the logical and the arbitrary has commonly been used by specialists in feats of memory.

If Mr Raven has a long nose, the practitioner imagines him with a huge bird in the middle of his face, and the recollection of Mr Raven is supposed to survive the fancy. The attempt to use this principle in a mechanical aid appears to be new.

20 January 1965

MOUSE HELPS TO LAY A CABLE

A mouse helped to lay a telephone cable under a railway level crossing at Lincoln today. It quickly accomplished what four men had pondered over for three days.

The problem was to pass the cable a distance of 32 ft through a narrow gap between a water main and the metal sheath enclosing it.

After unsuccessful attempts to thread the cable through, two of the workmen, Charles Lyon and Trevor Jackson, both of Boston, had an idea. Early this morning they caught three mice, which they took to work with them in a shoe box. They tied a strong thread round the tail of a mouse and slipped it into the gap.

The mouse ran forward but soon emerged at its starting point and had to be sent off again. This time the operation succeeded with a few gentle jerks on the thread when it stopped running. Mr Lyon fed the line out at one end and Mr Jackson, waiting at the other end, caught the mouse.

The thread was untied and pulled through the gap with a stronger piece of cord attached to it; and to the cord was fixed the telephone cable. In all, Operation Mouse had taken an hour and a half.

28 May 1965

INCONVENIENCE LIKE A FISH OUT OF WATER

A *Phocaena phocaena* was found today propped up in one of the cubicles of the men's lavatory in Glasgow Central station. The staff thought it was a dolphin, but the 4 ft

64 lb carcass was identified as a porpoise by the museums department at Kelvingrove Park.

How it had come into the lavatory nobody knew; one gentleman said: 'We had heavy rain and there was flooding, but this is ridiculous.'

It was taken to Glasgow City Council's museum and art galleries, where Mr Charles Palmer, curator of the Department of Natural History, said: 'It is a freshly caught porpoise. These are quite common in the Clyde. We are going to have a glass fibre cast taken of it.'

2 November 1965

BODY IN ICE WAITS FOR CANCER CURE

The body of Dr James Bedford, a retired university teacher, will arrive today packed in ice at Phoenix, Arizona. It will be frozen in liquid nitrogen in a capsule from which he hopes to emerge after a cure for cancer has been found.

Dr Bedford, aged 73, was declared clinically dead a week ago in Glendale, California. Knowing that he was suffering from incurable lung cancer, he had directed in his will that his body should be consigned to the Cryonics Society for the experiment.

Mr Raymond Vest, at whose home Dr Bedford was declared dead, said a team of three members of the Cryonics Society of Southern California led by Dr Dante Brunel, arrived at the dying man's bedside and began packing him in ice. They applied artificial respiration and external heart massage to keep the brain alive while the freezing process went on.

'They worked for eight hours freezing the body,' said Mr Vest. 'The doctor's widow was there and his son, Norman. We had to send Norman out for more ice once.'

20 January 1967

BOOMERANG'S BIG WHITE CHIEF

Frank Donellan, now 70, was only eight when King Billy, an old aboriginal chief in Botany Bay, first taught him how to throw a boomerang. Now, as holder of the world boomerang throwing championship for the past 37 years and pioneer of the modern boomerang, he has become the big white chief of this ancient Australian aboriginal art.

'These days I make their boomerangs for them and I've taught many of the dark blokes to throw them,' he said, chucking one across Hyde Park towards the Hilton hotel.

He laments the waning interest of aboriginals in the boomerang. 'The trouble is that the white man has taken over. Of course that is bad. But I've done my best. I've even tried to start an all-aboriginal game of boomerang base: something like baseball played with boomerang.'

Remaining Ambition

When Donellan takes his boomerangs – a boxful of all shapes and sizes – for a gallop, as he calls it, there is not much he cannot make them do. He can knock down a bird in flight, hurl a boomerang and catch it on the return blindfolded, or knock an apple off his head with a 300 ft round sweep. He even sets three or four in orbit at once.

Donellan says it was King Billy who taught him the art of carving a boomerang out of the angular trees in mangrove swamps, but he says he has vastly improved the aerodynamic aspects of the weapon since those days. These days his boomerangs are made of balsa wood and moulded from synthetic fabrics.

'One of my main helpers in making the modern boomerang was Charles Kingsford-Smith, the aviator. Before he died he commissioned me to make a boomerang to his specifications to test out theories on the construction of the aeroplane wing. That boomerang started me on a specific line of study and I have made a deep study of aerodynamics in relation to the boomerang since then. My present design is as good as you can get them.'

His remaining ambition is to be the first man to throw a boomerang in the Sydney Opera House.

2 April 1968

DARWIN'S THEORY ON APES CHALLENGED

by **Peter Nichols**

ROME All those children who asked for teddy bears this Christmas were supporting the theory of Dr Luigi Ammendola, a Neapolitan biologist, psychologist and palaeontologist, who has published a correction to Darwin with the object of showing that man's common ancestry was with bears and not monkeys.

Dr Ammendola accepts Darwin's views with the exception of what he feels to be this one slip of deciding for monkeys. The bear, he points out, has a great deal more in common with man.

Monkeys have little power of reflection, are garrulous and superficial. Man is more introvert, reserved and of 'carnivorous humour'.

Bears in their hunting adopt a system of division of labour unknown to monkeys. The bears have worked it out for themselves. No student of monkeys has ever noted that they work in partnership.

Dr Ammendola also points out that the sexual habits of bears are nearer to those of men. For instance, bears purposely send away their young when about to copulate: monkeys have far less of a sense of propriety.

Monkeys do not think of providing for the future. Once they have eaten enough bananas they simply leave the rest.

Dr Ammendola first began to evolve his theory when dealing with man's psychological habits. Human dreams always suggested to him an earthbound race, not one accustomed to living in the trees. When a man dreams of falling, for instance, it is of a fall while walking down the stairs or over a precipice – and not from a treetop.

A dream of flying is interpreted by Freudians as erotic,

'. . . more in common with man'
[DARWIN'S THEORY ON APES CHALLENGED]

but it is also, in Dr Ammendola's view, the typical dream of a species accustomed to swimming, which is valid for bears but not for monkeys.

The cave, not the tree, is man's maximum desire, as expressed in his need for a house: the lack of a roof is felt more than the lack of love. Monkeys on the other hand, are happy in the open.

Like birds, monkeys have a melodic sense. Awareness of changes in tone are essential to them for self-protection and for hunting because they need to be able to recognize the sounds of the wind, of the leaves and the approach of other animals.

Men and bears are born, instead, with a rhythmic sense, typical of animals that live by hunting their prey but are heavily built and not agile. They need perfect timing to deal with an advancing prey and to win with one blow.

To all these examples of psychology and habits in which man is nearer to the bear than the ape Dr Ammendola adds a series of anatomical comparisons between man and the bear.

His conclusion is simple. The distant ancestor of the bear was carnivorous and cave-dwelling, while that of the monkey was a herbivorous tree-dweller, and man belongs to the former rather than the latter line.

29 December 1969

PRODIGY AT TWO

MADRAS The Madras Music Academy has announced a monthly allowance for three years for the proper musical training of a two-year-old child, Ravikiran, said to be a prodigy. He is stated to be able to recite the 72 basic ragas or tunes of the Carnatic system of music.

2 January 1970

RUSSIAN LANGUAGE FINDS ITSELF INVADED BY REGBY, SVITERS, MR HIT, BIZNES, BITNIKS AND ALL THAT DZHAZ

by **David Bonavia**

Franglais and Japlish have already taken their places alongside the world's great languages. Russlish, which is perhaps less rich and up to date than either, nonetheless deserves attention for the ingenuity of its distortions.

The best specimen to appear so far is *Nokautirovat*, a boxing term meaning 'to knock out'. Then there is *irovat*, a verbal ending commonly attached to foreign loan-words, to indicate that there is no intention of paying them back.

Sporting terms lead the list of English borrowings in Russian, and have suffered indignities similar to those inflicted on them by French. Not content with *futbol*, the Russians now also play *regby*, but *kriket* has never acquired a following.

Since a sportsman is a *sportsmen*, sportsmen have to be *sportsmeny*, and a sportswoman is a *sportsmenka* (plural *sportsmenki*). Similarly a businessman is a *biznesmen* – a somewhat derogatory term in Russian. Anyone who conducts a *biznes* in the Soviet Union is dealing on the black market.

A *dzehntelmen*, surprisingly, still commands respect in Russia, and a *ledy* is invariably the wife of a lord. So it causes amusement when an English speaking person calls an ordinary woman a lady.

In returning to sport, every *futbolist* wants to win his *mach* (not to be confused with the Russian word *myach* meaning a ball), the *atlets* are taught by *treners* to run on *treks*, and a distinguished sportsman is given the title of *master* – normally a term of respect for a plumber, electrician, piano tuner or hairdresser, male or female.

As in the case of most languages, borrowings from English are mostly recent. The Russians began by borrowing from the Finns (many place names including Moskva), then got in debt to the Greeks (for religious terms), the Turks (for a miscellany of things connected with horses, tents, and so on), the French (for the whole caboodle of socio-political jargon), and the Germans (for science, industry, mechanics and warfare).

The English with their complex sports, and the Irish with their *huligany* (hooligans), have been overtaken by the Americans with their cultural decadence, reflected in such Russian words as *dzhaz* (jazz), *bitnik* and *hippi*. *Bitnik*, by the way, has a feminine form: *bitnitsa*. American cities are *dzhungli* (jungles). However, American industry has contributed *buldozer*, which has lost an 'l' on the way.

Mercifully, the Russians have begun to drop the use of G to transliterate the English H, which has made Hamlet irretrievably Gamlet. Mr Heath is now Mr Hit, instead of Mr Gif as he might have been 50 years ago.

People wear *dzhempers* (jumpers), and *sviters* (sweaters). The French and the Germans have misled the Russians into believing that a dinner jacket is called a *smoking*, but this does not matter much because no one wears such a thing in the Soviet Union – except concert pianists, waiters and foreigners.

You may go up in a *lift* to attend a *miting*, where *pamflets* will be handed round. There is a *risk* that your place of work may be subject to a *raid* (a spot check on efficiency or book-keeping).

Each five-year plan gets off to a *start* – a sporting term which has been taken over to encourage keenness among the workers. With any luck the plan can be brought to a successful *finish* a month or two ahead of schedule. Then everyone can drink a *tost*.

21 June 1971

COLD ON TOES CURES COLD IN NOSE

Two Israeli scientists say they have invented a machine that cures the common cold. But some doubt is being felt by other scientists at the annual meeting of the Society for Cryobiology.

Dr Aladar Schwartz of the Israel Institute of Technology in Haifa, one of the inventors, said in a scientific paper co-authored by Dr Menachem Ram of the Rothschild Hospital in Haifa that more than 100 people had been cured by application of intense cold to the undersides of their big toes.

Dr Schwartz, an engineer, said he wasn't sure why the 'cold cure' works, but not a single failure had been recorded. He cited the case of a 15-year-old boy who was cured of sniffles that plagued him for years.

Dr Schwartz was reluctant to provide details of the machine, as patents are pending. But he said Dr Ram believes the treatment may be akin to the Chinese use of acupuncture – in which each part of the body is thought to have an opposite number which, if penetrated with needles, will relieve discomfort in its 'partner'.

4 September 1971

[A low-technology version of this technique, in which the big toes are placed on an ice-tray straight from a domestic refrigerator, gave promising results. Could the effects be analogous to those produced by that old-fashioned remedy, in which the nerves are stimulated by heat – the mustard bath?]

PRIESTLEY ARTICLE SETS OFF STORM IN AN EGGCUP

by **Michael Leapman**

An article about eggs by J. B. Priestley, published this month in *The New York Times*, has provoked a correspondence of a ferocity and boiling passion seldom equalled. The letters, which take up more than half the newspaper's features page today, are fresh proof that nothing divides Britain and the United States so much as their food.

The Priestley article, a shortened version of a piece that appeared originally in the *New Statesman*, was about brown and white eggs. It led to a long correspondence in *The Times*. The author made the point that, although the British preferred brown eggs, Americans despised them, sold them off cheaply and sometimes threw them away, preferring the white variety.

He believed that this was because white eggs suggested hygiene and purity. It was, he said, a symptom of the weakness of American civilization, which he called 'a bloodless extrapolation of a satisfying life'. As a further instance he asserted that Americans discover sex from manuals instead of in bed.

As all who write about America know, you cannot make such remarks with impunity, especially if you are British. The tone of today's correspondence was set by the first letter, from Erica Jong, of New York.

The article was, she said, 'a perfect example of English jingoism disguised as social comment'. It was amazing that any contemporary writer could begin a paragraph with the phrase 'We English' or 'Here in England' without intending irony. 'He sounds like something invented by Jonathan Swift to satirize the English,' she wrote.

Marion Hart, from Washington, attacked both Mr Priestley and the English cuisine at a stroke. 'If he thinks he is profound he is silly. If he thinks he is funny he is naive,' she spluttered.

'Anyone who has thrived for so many years on a diet of boiled mutton, Brussels sprouts and soggy fried potatoes can hardly qualify as an expert on good living. But why do you have to print this stuff?'

Some correspondents disputed Mr Priestley's facts. Brown eggs were not cheaper than white, they claimed. Several made the point that in the north-eastern states brown eggs were preferred and more expensive – perhaps why the region is called New England.

Others accepted the validity of the facts but not of Mr Priestley's interpretation of them. Joseph Moore, of New York, told a wounded story of how, in Rhodes, an Englishman had criticized him for tipping too heavily, saying he would 'spoil the natives for the rest of us'.

29 December 1971

SMOKE, DRINK AND LIVE TO 142

Dr David Davies of London Univeristy is going back to Ecuador today to explore further the possibilities of living to 140. He will revisit the valley of Vilcabamba, where last year he discovered a group of inhabitants who thought nothing of living to 100. The oldest was 142 and his age was verified by a baptismal certificate.

Davies described his find in an article in *New Scientist* in February. He said at a press conference yesterday that a possible reason for the long lives of Vilcabambans was their low-calorie diet. Their average daily intake of calories is 1,700, half the average in Britain. They eat only one ounce of meat a week.

'. . . four cups of rum'
[SMOKE, DRINK AND LIVE TO 142]

Certainly abstemiousness is no part of the reason. The people drink two to four cups of rum and smoke between 40 and 60 cigarettes a day. The valley is tranquil and the climate mild, which may have something to do with why they live so long. The locals themselves think it is because of the herbal teas they drink.

Another theory Davies advanced yesterday was that there could be a trace element in the soil which accounted for long life, since the people of Vilcabamba grow their own vegetables in the valley. Some think this is the reason for Britain's own oasis of longevity on the Norfolk coast, where people reach 100 more often than elsewhere.

Gerontology is Davies's special subject. There are other valleys where people live a long time in Georgia in the Soviet Union, and in Pakistan. In Thailand there are places where folk age quickly, where people of 37 look 67. . .

He said yesterday that he was returning to Ecuador as a matter of urgency. Asked why it was urgent, he said he wanted to complete his research before hordes of other scholars and tourists tramped over the area. He might have added that he is already 44, and life is short.

19 April 1973

MAN WALKS ON TOP OF NEW YORK

A Frenchman today defied winds and the police to walk a tightrope between the second tallest buildings in the world, the 1,350 ft twin towers of the World Trade Centre in New York.

Philippe Petit, aged 24, of Nemours, a professional stunt man, walked back and forth between the two 110-storey towers above the streets of Manhattan's financial district as hundreds of people below watched.

He crossed the 90 ft span several times, stopping now and then to lie on the wire or wiggle a foot, while dozens of policemen gathered on the roof of each building.

In 1971 M Petit walked between the towers of Notre Dame Cathedral in Paris and last year he walked across a wire slung between the two towers of the Sydney Harbour Bridge.

One of the first to see the stunt was Mr Richie Santiago, a guard at the centre. He said he had to report the walk to officials and the police several times before anyone would believe him.

When the police finally reacted, they did so in force, sending their special emergency squad to the centre. Police officers argued with M Petit for several minutes during which M Petit stayed carefully out of reach.

When he ended his stunt, according to one witness, 'he almost ran across the wire' into the waiting arms of the police.

He was immediately arrested, handcuffed with an alleged accomplice, and taken to a psychiatric hospital ward for observation.

Charges were not immediately made because no one seemed sure what charges were possible.

A police officer said it must have taken M Petit three days to get his equipment to the top. Machinery was needed to 'shoot' his cable from one tower to another and stretch it.

A spokesman at Beekman Hospital said M Petit and his assistant, M Jean Francois Heckel, aged 25, were found to be in 'excellent health, both physically and psychologically'.

'They were exuberant and delighted with what they accomplished,' he added. . .

M Petit's feat almost doubled the previous record for the highest tightrope walk. The *Guinness Book of Records* lists the walk of Karl Wallenda over the 750ft Tallulah Gorge in Georgia, United States, as the previous record.

The two men were later taken to Ericcson Place police station. Police said it had finally been decided to charge them with criminal trespass and disorderly conduct.

8 August 1974

PETS' CABIN

Although [Patent] BP1 382 079 from Aubrey Brockhouse of Illinois, in the United States, may seem an elaborate solution to a simple problem, it could be welcomed by city dwellers owning pets.

A small cabin is secured over a domestic drain and mains water supply plumbed into a small storage tank like a cistern. Inside the cabin there is a treadle board on which the animal is toilet-trained to stand.

This causes the board to move down from a tilted to a flat position, which operates the first stage of a two-stage valve. When the animal moves off the board and out of the cabin the board tilts up again and releases the second stage of the valve, dousing the slope of the board with flushing water.

7 May 1975

FISH BEHAVIOUR: KEEPING IN TOUCH

It is an axiom of ethologists who turn their attention to human studies that for any human behaviour a counterpart will be found in the animal kingdom. The reverse is not true; nature maintains a clear lead in bizarre relationships – witness the extraordinary sexual bondage of the males of certain species of anglerfish. Recent investigations have shown that such is the anxiety of the fish to establish a lasting sexual relationship that it is not only parasitic but frequently precocious.

The fish in question are ceratoid anglerfish that live at depths of 500 metres or more in all the world's oceans. Since the population of the anglerfish is very thinly spread out, opportunities for reproductive meetings must be very rare. Once contact has been made it is clearly to the advantage of the species if the relationship can be made permanent.

It has been known for many years that the male anglerfish has, at the tips of his jaws, a set of pincer-like teeth that he sinks into the female on meeting, never to let go. In the ensuing months the male slowly fuses with his mate.

At first it is only the topmost layers of cells around the jaws of the male that become continuous with the corresponding female epidermis. But gradually the fusion becomes more extensive until, although the male's body is still to be seen, it has appended to the female to such an extent that even the blood systems of the two fish are connected. By then it is no longer necessary for the male to eat, because his requirements can be fully met through his mate's bloodstream. In return the female seeks nothing but sperm, on tap.

The apotheosis of the male's testicles is at the expense of his general development. While he may start off at about the same size as the female, a full grown female of 300 millimetres can be 20 times the size of the attached male. At that stage the testes may occupy the whole of the body cavity of the male, while other organs such as the eye become mere relics of the organs they used to be.

Dr Theodore Pietsch, of the Museum of Comparative Zoology at Harvard University, has described in a recent issue of *Nature* two recently captured couples of the angler fish *Cryptopsaras couesi* that have turned out to be the smallest and youngest examples yet known. From the size of the fish and the sexual immaturity of the females, the age can be estimated as not more than 12 months. Since their fusion is already well advanced, the initial meeting of the fish must have been very early in their lives.

An analysis of all the recorded specimens of *C. couesi* reveals that they consist of 200 free living females, 75 free living males and only nine fused couples. The relative scarcity of couples emphasizes how important it is that such rare meetings that do occur are not allowed to be just brief encounters, however young the fish. Dr Pietsch is clearly correct in believing that his discovery of the precocity of sexual parasitism in the anglerfish 'makes this solution to the seemingly difficult problem of reproduction in the deep sea, even more remarkable'.

9 July 1975

COLONEL SAW RED WITH THE WHISTLING LIBRARIAN

by **Dan van der Vat**

BONN A legal battle over the right of the chief librarian of the West German Defence Ministry to whistle the 'Internationale' in the corridor has been settled out of court, it was disclosed in Bonn today.

The facts in the case are that on 29 March the librarian, Dr Folker Hansen, was heard whistling the revolutionary song, among other tunes, by Colonel Alois Friedel of the Defence Staff.

The colonel at once forbade Dr Hansen to repeat the 'offence', then went to the librarian's superior and demanded disciplinary proceedings against him, his suspension and his transfer out of the ministry.

In self-defence, the whistling librarian lodged a complaint against the colonel for abusing his authority. Dr Hansen, a Christian Democrat town councillor in a municipality near Bonn, also wrote a letter of protest to a local newspaper which appeared on 21 May.

The key passage read: 'Thirty-one years after the destruction of fascism in Germany, we are apparently again at the stage where even active democrats are defamed as leftist extremists because they whistle tunes which others do not like.'

Colonel Friedel's response to this was to lodge a complaint at the state attorney's office alleging insulting behaviour and also to bring an action in the Bonn state court seeking a temporary injunction against Dr Hansen to stop him making any more public statements.

The librarian had also accused the colonel of suppressing free expression of opinion, lacking the democratic spirit and failing to respect the fundamental principles of leadership.

The civil court sat for five hours. Dr Hansen's lawyer argued that he had drawn valid conclusions about the colonel's attitude from his behaviour. The colonel's lawyer argued that the case had nothing to do with whistling the 'Internationale' but only with the alleged insults.

The court declared the case closed and took no further action when Dr Hansen made a statement that he had not intended to accuse Colonel Friedel of 'Nazi methods', and the colonel in turn undertook to withdraw his complaint of insulting behaviour. The colonel is to pay two-thirds of the undisclosed costs of the hearing.

5 June 1976

SLOW DAY FOR NEWS

by **Clive Borrell**

It was a slow news day so I telephoned the Yard. 'Sorry, there is very little crime about.'

I grunted and wondered whether to write out my expenses. 'I can offer you a flying pink pig if you like.'

I grunted again. 'I see those every morning,' I said.

'Really. There's a flying pink pig loose at 7,000 feet and it's causing a hazard to aircraft.'

I told him to look at his calendar. 'There are months to go before April 1,' I said.

Twenty minutes later I decided to ring someone else at the Yard. 'Not much about I'm afraid unless you're interested in a flying pink pig,' he said, and laughed.

'Do you want me to tell you about it?' I knew I was not going to get any peace until he did.

'At 10.25 this morning a pink pig balloon measuring 10 metres by five metres, escaped from its mooring in the car park of Battersea power station. It was there to advertise the pop group, Pink Floyd, but it broke loose.

'One of our helicopters on traffic patrol intercepted a radio message from a light aircraft to the control tower at Heathrow airport. The pilot was heard to say: "I've just been overtaken by a pink elephant at 7,000 feet."

'The helicopter crew offered to help because the control tower could not plot the creature on their radar.'

He paused. 'Don't tell me – you chased it,' I said in disbelief. 'No, we escorted it across London as far as Crystal Palace. Now it's out of our area,' he said regretfully.

At noon the helium balloon was 20 miles east of London over the Essex suburbs and the Civil Aviation Authority was also infected by mirth.

Later police in Essex reported: 'It's at about 5,000 feet and seems to be coming down. It must be getting hungry.' I groaned. I gave up grunting when I realized the significance of the noise.

By mid-afternoon the pig was 18,000 feet above Chatham, and gave every appearance of heading home to Germany, where it was made.

But several hours later it became deflated and subsided disconsolately on to a farm at Chilham, near Canterbury.

4 December 1976

BUNBURY BY ANY OTHER NAME . . .

It was, as Wilde might have said, the unconstrainable in pursuit of the unattainable. But I am getting ahead of myself . . .

The dignified notification was headed: Francis Bunberry Scholarships. A copy went to the president at every junior common room at Oxford. The Bunberry Trust, it said, offered three scholarships to enable undergraduates to travel – all expenses paid – within the Commonwealth and America.

Successful applicants would attend courses on a wide range of subjects and meet people from all walks of life.

More than 100 applied. They sent their thickly worded application forms to the trust, c/o the Grosvenor House Hotel in London, as requested on the notification.

Meanwhile, the trust contacted the Randolph Hotel in Oxford booking dinner for more than 40 of the students it would select for interview. It also booked rooms for the interviewers, and for interviewees.

In not a single mind, academic or catering, was there a shadow of doubt. Not, that is, until there was a thundering silence from the trustees.

Which is not surprising, considering there are no Bunberry scholarships, no trustees and no trust.

The hoaxer's identity is not known. But there is a clue, of sorts. In *The Importance of Being Earnest* the philandering Algernon Moncrieff dreams up a permanent invalid behind whose coat tails he can hide when in deceitful mood. His name is Bunbury.

9 March 1978

No editions of The Times *appeared between 30 November 1978 and 13 November 1979.*

THE DIFFICULTY OF BEING THE SECOND SALVADOR DALI

by **Harry Debelius**

It would be hard to take Salvador Dali seriously if it were not for his painting. With his clown-like gestures and his antenna moustache, he hardly seems to take himself seriously. Yet there is something very serious indeed about this modern master painter whose 75th year is now being celebrated.

His habit of talking in riddles, of pausing for effect, or making facile pronouncements on transcendental issues is disconcerting. Some think it is all a facade. In fact it is not entirely put on. As Dali revealed for the first time in a recent magazine interview, he has spent much of his life trying to convince himself of his own identity.

'I had a brother who died of meningitis when he was five years old, before I was born,' Dali told Carlos Pedregal of Spain's mass-circulation weekly *Interviu*. 'Since my parents were very fond of him, they gave me his name: he was called Salvador Dali. And they treated me as if I were the other one.

'We would be talking along the street for example and they would say to me, "The other one sneezed when he passed by here, be careful." Or they were forever repeating things like how good-looking he was and the like.

'Then I wasn't me. I was the dead one. Whenever I went into my parents' room and saw the photo of my dead brother I couldn't sleep because my head was full of ideas of putrefaction and death. They scared me terrifically. The thought of my brother was anguishing. Even today I'm anguished by it.

'I've had a constant struggle to affirm my own personality, to overcome the frightening thought that I was really dead. So I had to resort to all kinds of eccentricities, put loaves of bread on my head, crawl on all fours and things like that. Every odd thing I did was done to kill my dead brother and prove that I wasn't him, that I was the living one.'

19 May 1980

DAMN, THERE GOES ANOHTER

by **Philip Howard**

Chaps who live in glass houses shouldn't throw stones. Hacks for daily newspapers who joke about misprints, or, as we call them in the trade, literals, are chucking hand grenades about in the tropical house at Kew. I had a letter the other day from one of the great ladies of the English theatre, pointing out five literals in a piece I had written,

'. . . all kinds of eccentricities'
[THE DIFFICULTY OF BEING THE SECOND SALVADOR DALI]

and remarking more in sorrow than in anger that it would not have done in the days before the First World War, when her husband worked in the sub-editors' room of *The Times*.

I wrote back defensively . . . new technology . . . teething troubles . . . more words in *The Times* than in three novels of average length . . . don't start writing them until after lunch, and you know what journalists' lunches are reputed to be . . . daily miracle on your breakfast table . . . meaning matters more than misprints . . . will try to do better.

Of course, we should like to print *The Times* perfectly without blemish or literal. But in the daily Niagara of journalism it is never going to happen. It never did. There is a myth that, in the golden days before some war or another, *The Times* paid a shilling to any reader who cut out and sent in a misprint. Poppycock, like the myth about sleeping all night in the Chamber of Horrors.

It is true that Lord Northcliffe made us keep £50 in gold at the front desk, after a reporter missed a scoop because there was no money in Printing House Square; and it is true that in the bad old days of exploitation, when the paper was much smaller and more heavily manned, a linotype-operator had a penny docked from his wages for every literal in his copy. But there have always been marvellous misprints in *The Times*.

The most famous was the report of Queen Victoria opening the Menai Bridge, in which, instead of 'the Queen then passed over the bridge', we had her doing something more *insouciant*. My own favourite was in the learned piece about the Dead Sea Scrolls, dictated from out of town, which referred to them throughout and in every edition as 'the Dead Sea Squirrels'.

I liked the one the other day in which our learned Agriculture Correspondent referred to rare breeds of cattle having 'carving' difficulties: apt, because as well as having trouble giving birth, they tend to be as tough as old boots.

Geoffrey Dawson, when editor, himself caught in the first edition 'Queen Mary has graciously promised to send her face for exhibition'. It was lace she had promised to send. In the 1920s a compositor with a grievance inserted in a seven-column report of a Parliamentary speech the line: 'The Speaker then said he felt inclined for a bit of . . .,' attributing to the Prime Minister unusual candour for the House of Commons.

Dear Philip Hope-Wallace of *The Guardian* was the Professor of the Misprint. There was his account of *The Merchant of Venice* with Olivier as Skylark; there was his review of *Doris Godunov*; there was his notice of *La Traviata*: 'The music hall direction was in the capable hands of . . .' He finished dictating a notice: 'The programme had begun with an admirable performance of Elgar's overture *In the South*.' End (sc. *finis*). This appeared as 'Elgar's overture *In Southend*'. His own favourite concerned his description of Tosca as being 'like a tigress robbed of her whelps'.

The editor, a feminist, changed 'tigress' into 'tiger'. The printer, on his own initiative, changed 'whelps' into 'whelks'. So Tosca appeared 'like a tiger robbed of his whelks'.

Of course misprints are not a laughing matter. We bleed when they appear in our copy. They irritate. Sometimes they obscure the meaning, which is the Sin against the Word. But on occasions they have Surrealist poetry, and add to the gaiety of nations.

And yes, of course, we shall try to do better. Now, Mr Chief Sub-Editor, Mr Printer, and Mr Compositor, let's see what you can make of that bit of copy. Japs who live in farmhouses shouldn't stow thrones.

8 October 1982

WOMAN'S BODY EATEN BY CATS

STONEHAM, MASSACHUSETTS The remains of an 84-year-old woman, described as a cat lover who took in abandoned animals, were eaten by dozens of her pets after she died of natural causes.

'The body was in a semi-skeletal state,' a police officer said. 'It was one of the roughest things I've ever seen. They were feeding off her.' Cats living in the house attacked officers who tried to recover the body of Hilda Diggdon. They were removed and destroyed.

5 November 1982

LAST OF THE OLD-TIME HOODLUMS

by **Christopher Thomas**

NEW YORK Meyer Lansky, the financial 'godfather' of organized crime, is dead. The last of the old-time hoodlums succumbed to cancer on Saturday at the age of 81, ending a legendary career of murder, theft and intrigue.

He died at the Mount Sinai Hospital close to the Miami apartment block where he spent his later years. The underworld, no doubt, is bereft. He was to many of today's young crime bosses an inspiration, a charismatic super-crook who dodged the law for 60 years.

For decades he was reputedly a leading figure in Murder Inc. and was probably a paid assassin in the 1920s, although for the past half a century he had others do the dirty work while he exploited his penchant for financial manipulation.

Lansky was one of the biggest bootleggers. He had a multi-million dollar gambling empire in Cuba until Dr Castro cracked down on the slot machine and roulette tables.

He operated a loan shark operation in which a swift, final judgment was passed on defaulters and he led organized crime into the legitimate world of business, penetrating well-established companies and setting up new ones with underworld money.

The police and the Federal Bureau of Investigation tried

for decades to nail him but he spent only two months in jail. That was in 1953 on a minor charge of running an illegal gambling house, and he treated the experience like the joke it patently was.

Maler Suchowijanski, a Russian born immigrant, changed his name early. He spent a wretched childhood in New York's Lower East Side but his teachers at Public School 34 remembered him as totally self-possessed. Within five years of leaving school he was working as a mechanic, repairing and disguising stolen cars for bootleggers.

Legend has it that Lansky and Lucky Luciano were enlisted by the Office of Naval Intelligence during the Second World War to get underworld assistance in tracing German and Italian secret agents in New York. It is said that because of his valuable help a deportation order was dropped against Lansky.

In the 1960s his empire was so great that he kept a former bootlegging associate in Switzerland as his full-time money manager. He decided in 1970 to retire to Israel, which prompted a long legal battle which resulted in a refusal to let him stay because he was 'a danger to public safety'.

Finally he came home to Florida and was arrested on a variety of charges. 'That's life,' he said. 'At my age it's too late to worry. What will be will be. A Jew has a slim chance in the world.'

17 January 1983

THE TALK OF THE TOWER GETS THE BIRD

by **Paul Pickering**

As Labour MPs ask angry questions about American bases and the exact number of United States servicemen in the country, one creature could be of great help. Hector the Raven had a sixth sense in his days at the Bloody Tower that could spot a dawdling tourist from the Land of the Free at half a mile.

First, the tourist heard a beating of wings and then looked around to see the bird's hideous talons, piercing eyes and long sharp beak. But when it said 'Hello, c'mon then' in an aggressive Arthur Mullard voice, sheer panic set in.

Brought up on a diet of horror movies like *The Exorcist* and *Omen II*, there are still deeply-shocked citizens from places like Little Rock who believe the devil is alive and well and living in the Tower of London.

Hector, the talking raven, worked very hard for years to make London a tourist-free zone, reserving particular venom for Americans, ripping the windscreen wipers off their limousines and stealing sweets from their children.

Now, possibly to save the Special Relationship, Hector has been incarcerated in London Zoo where I adopted him this week and, under the zoo's highly successful scheme, will help keep their only political prisoner in rats for a year: 'He was never a bad lad when I was around,' said Yeoman Raven Master John Wilmington of the Tower. 'He was just a bit high spirited really.

'He would have a go at anything from a Bentley to a guardsman's boots. He just assumed that everything belonged to him. But I fed him and made friends with him and he would sit on my shoulder.'

. . . Yet Hector does have a sense of humour. 'He hides a sixpence in his cage,' said Fred. 'When someone comes along he talks to them and then fetches the sixpence and passes it through the bars. They think this is wonderful and pass it back. Then he bites them.' He thinks this great fun and bounces round his cage laughing and shouting, 'What you got there then?' as the person is led away for first aid.

But Hector has a tender side too; he is devoted to Doris. 'No one is quite certain that she is female,' said Fred. 'But she must be because Hector would have killed another male. They bill and coo and he is teaching her to talk.'

Sarah Chivers, the bright young lady who runs the adoption service, looked at me curiously: 'No one else has wanted to adopt Hector,' she said. This must have been the reaction Normal Mailer got when he befriended Gary Gilmore.

'We have a Mr and Mrs Bat who adopted a fruit bat, a Miss Taper a tapir and a Mrs Squirrel who adopted a pygmy hippo. The LSE students' union has the left half of a beaver and the unemployment office at Battersea has adopted an orang-utan, but no one asked about Hector.

'One man adopted a bird-eating spider because he said his wife was crazy about spiders, and the wife of a gossip columnist got him a carpet python. The only trouble comes when they ask to take them home for the weekend,' said Sarah. But Hector is not so much on show as sentenced, doing bird as it were.

'The ravens came to London at the time of the plague and stayed,' said John Wilmington. 'When the residents eventually petitioned Charles II to get rid of them his soothsayer told him that if he did his palace would crumble to dust.'

It is obvious from the legend that the Tower Ravens, not least Hector, provide a valuable and patriotic defence against nuclear attack, pestilences, inundations, tourism and the like, and to stand down this deterrent and imprison its leader is very dangerous.

It's surely about time that the GLC gave the odd thousand pounds or so to Ravens Against American Tourism to help them study ways that Hector's remaining comrades can bring an end to the problem.

Or, as Hector tells me that he is just as vigilant against Russian tourists, perhaps Mr Heseltine could employ him instead of cruise against the Ruskies. But until he regains his former glory I shall keep the jolly fellow supplied with rats.

10 March 1983

DRACULA SYNDROME

Two psychiatrists in Cape Town have written a paper for

the *South African Medical Journal* which suggests that a possible murder motive overlooked in the past is a bizarre desire to drink blood.

Dr R. E. Hemphill and Dr T. Zabow report in detail on three cases where white middle-class males, not apparently of Transylvanian origin, have had this craving, satisfied only by taking blood from animals when still alive, or after death from the abattoirs, or by sucking blood from the necks and shoulders of their lovers. Denied these sources, they have cut their arms and wrists to drink their own blood.

In a review of these and other cases, who have attended Cape Town University's psychiatric department, they report that although women are inclined to be auto-vampires, usually drinking their own blood, men are tempted to take other people's. They cite Haigh, the acid bath murderer, as a classic vampirist; it is known that he murdered nine people, cut their throats and drank a cupful of blood from each.

Vampirists are preoccupied with death and the dead. Even as small children they have an obsessive desire to visit cemeteries in a search for bodies and bones, and keep dead animals in their bedrooms.

The report suggests that this yearning may lead to repeated assaults or unexplained murder and should be considered in assessing the record of violent criminals who show evidence of self-mutilation.

6 May 1983

EVEN MORE BULL

Readers who have been inundating me with that word which means 'the carousing of seamen on an icebound ship'* and who know about my newfound delight in

* Mallemaroking – not Alphsbulling as one reader suggested.

'. . . behind a waterfall'
[EVEN MORE BULL]

obscure words, will not be surprised if I take this opportunity of recommending our politicians a spot of taghairm. This, as several correspondents have pointed out and the new Chambers dictionary confirms, is 'inspiration sought by lying in a bullock's hide behind a waterfall'. A bit more of it and this country might never have come to this present pass.

10 May 1983

HEDGEHOG FLAVOUR OUT OF FAVOUR

Hedgehog-flavoured crisps have been banned from the menu of a mid-Wales public house: not as a matter of bad taste, more as a matter of bad description.

So now chemists at Wolverhampton Polytechnic are trying to develop a flavouring that will meet the local council's requirements for products labelled 'hedgehog flavour'.

Mr Philip Lewis and his wife stopped hedgehog crisp production in their kitchen at The Vaults, at Welshpool, after Powys County Council's trading standards department had a sample tested by the public analyst. He reported no trace of hedgehog in the product.

Mr Lewis was warned that he faced prosecution for a breach of the Trade Descriptions Act and, as a compromise, he has agreed to drop the word 'flavour' from his crisp bags so he can resume production.

Meanwhile, he has asked his brother, a lecturer at Wolverhampton Polytechnic, to ask the chemists to find a hedgehog flavouring to meet the law's requirements.

Mr Lewis said yesterday: 'The big companies all use flavouring for their crisps. There is no beef and onion in a packet of beef and onion crisps.

'Our crisps started as a joke, because we have several gypsy customers who kept asking if we sold hedgehog-flavoured crisps. I surprised them one night by producing a packet, but the thing snowballed because they became so popular.

'But I never dreamed anyone would seriously think we were using hedgehogs in them. We have some old gypsies in Welshpool who used to eat baked hedgehogs, and they have told me the flavour is somewhere between veal and pork. That is what the scientists are aiming for.

'If they come up with a suitable flavouring, we will consider putting it in the crisps if it is economically viable. We have been using herbs, and the crisps became very popular. One wholesaler wanted 60 boxes a week.'

24 September 1983

SIC TRANSIT GLORIA MONEY

by **John Earle**

ROME Do you need *consiliarium adversus inflationem* (a consultant against inflation)?

Fideuram, the financial consultancy subsidiary of the Italian state-owned lending institute IMI (Instituto Mobiliare Italiano), has taken a quarter page in the Vatican newspaper, *Osservatore Romano*, for the first advertisement in Latin by an Italian banking group.

The reader's eye is caught by a photograph of a young, bespectacled *consiliarius nummarius* (Financial adviser) showing his papers to a middle-aged man in an armchair. '*Et tu?*' it asks underneath. You could join the *ducenta undecim milia attentorum pecuniae servatorum* (the 211,000 careful preservers of their wealth) who are already being served through the group's *trecenta agrentariae* (300 banking branches).

All you have to do is *sume elenchum telephonicum* (take the telephone directory) and seek the nearest branch, and you will be visited *sine ulla obligatione* (without any obligation) by a consultant *in domo tua* (in your home).

The group has evidently chosen the pages of the *Osservatore*, whose 50,000 copies circulate among churchmen of many nationalities, to reach readers used in the past to dealing with the Vatican Bank, the Istituto per le Opere di Religione (IOR).

18 October 1983

CLEAN SWEEP

Fired by this (PHS) column's obvious partiality to mongoose stories, Dr Georges Ware of the Department of Bacteriology, University of Bristol, is the latest to declare himself. Mongooses are expensive pets, he reminds me, not only because of the delight they take in unpotting house plants, but also because 'no mongoose-proof bag clasp has yet been devised'. His very own Mingle was keen on cigarettes, which she would ferret out unerringly and destroy. But 'perhaps her most memorable and expensive excursion was the day she climbed our chimney, crossed the roof tops and came down the chimney of a house several doors away appearing, covered in soot, during a dinner party. Not satisfied with having scared the wits out of the diners and dusted each one evenly with soot, she sampled their dinner and then returned home by the same route and demanded that I bath her at once.' Mongle, Mingle's mate, was even worse, my correspondent adds. The mind bongles.

25 October 1983

INDEX OF HEADLINES

INDEX OF TOPICS

ACKNOWLEDGEMENTS

Thanks are due to the news agencies listed below for permission to include the articles listed:

REUTER
Cheaper Atomic Energy – President Peron's Claim
A Coelacanth Identified
£100,000 Fraud
Man Walks on Top of New York (Reuter, UPI and AP)

NEW YORK TIMES NEWS SERVICE
Cold on Toes Cures Cold in Nose

Permission to reproduce any of these articles in this book except for purposes of comment or review is needed from the relevant news agency as well as from *The Times*.

I would also like to thank Suzanna Powers for her editorial help; and both the London Library and the St. Pancras Library for their kind assistance in the research and preparation of this book.